# AMERICAN
# PICTURE
# PALACES

# AMERICAN PICTURE PALACES

## THE ARCHITECTURE OF FANTASY

### DAVID NAYLOR

**VNR** VAN NOSTRAND REINHOLD COMPANY
new york   cincinnati   toronto   london   melbourne

Published by Van Nostrand Reinhold Company
135 West 50th Street
New York, NY 10020

Van Nostrand Reinhold Limited
1410 Birchmount Road
Scarborough, Ontario M1P 2E7, Canada

Van Nostrand Reinhold Australia Pty. Ltd.
17 Queen Street
Mitcham, Victoria 3132, Australia

Van Nostrand Reinhold Company Limited
Molly Millars Lane
Wokingham, Berkshire, England

16 15 14 13 12 11 10 9 8 7 6 5 4 3 2 1

**Library of Congress Cataloging in Publication Data**

Naylor, David, 1955–
    American picture palaces.

    Bibliography: p.
    Includes index.
    1. Moving-picture theaters—United States.   I. Title.
NA6846.U6N39        725′.822′0973        81-10344
ISBN 0-442-23861-4                    AACR2

This book is dedicated to Brother Andrew Corsini
for his friendship, endless support, and eternal good humor.

And to friends and family for refuge along the way.

# CONTENTS

# PHOTO CREDITS

My deep appreciation to the following individuals and organizations for the use of photographic material:

Theatre Historical Society (THS): 5, 14r, 16t, 16b, 24l, 24r, 25l, 25r, 26, 27t, 27b, 34, 35l, 35r, 42t, 42b, 52tl, 52tr, 55tr, 60, 62, 68, 70t, 71t, 71b, 78, 79b, 91tl, 91tr, 100t, 100b, 104, 105t, 106t, 106b, 121b, 123t, 130, 133b, 134, 135, 136r, 140, 142, 147t, 161, 168, 169, 170, 171, 178, 180, 184, 186t, 186b, 197t, 197b, 198, 200b, 207

Terry Helgesen Collection, THS: 17, 18, 28, 66, 84, 85t, 87, 88, 97, 105br, 115, 118r, 120, 143tr, 144, 154, 155, 156t, 156b, 163, 164, 166t, 209

Ben Hall Collection, THS: 14l, 15, 39t, 39b, 41, 72, 76, 77, 80–81, 82b, 83, 86, 89tl, 112, 113, 114b, 116, 117, 119b, 129b, 136l, 138, 139l, 145, 146tl, 175, 187t, 189, 205

Chicago Architectural Photographing Company Collection, THS: 23, 36, 37t, 37b, 43t, 43bl, 43br, 46, 47, 48, 57, 58, 59t, 59b, 61t, 61b, 79b, 98r, 99, 101, 102, 103, 110t, 110b, 111t, 111b, 114t, 131, 132t, 132b, 137, 139r, 159, 160, 174, 176, 199, 202

Loew's Collection, THS: 12, 33t, 33b, 38t, 38b, 40, 45t, 45b, 70b, 73, 75t, 75b, 119t, 121t, 125, 126, 127, 128t, 128b, 129t, 158, 203

Brother Andrew Corsini, THS: 81b, 82t, 90tl, 90b, 98l, 118l, 123b, 146tr, 148t, 162

Bill Peterson Collection, THS: 165t, 165b

Bret Eddy, THS: 53b

Frank Cronican, THS: 55b

Steve Levin, THS: 166b, 167t, 185t

Michael Miller, THS: 188tr

William Kluver, THS: 94t

James C. Kogel, THS: 148b

Fred Beall Collection, THS: 213

Miles Rudisill Collection, THS: 133t

William C. Frisk, THS: 93l

Los Angeles Public Library, THS: 143tl, 143b, 204, 208, 212t, 212b

Utah State Historical Society, THS: 85b

Francis LaCloche, THS: 157

Lud Keaton, Arizona Republic, THS: 153

D. R. Goff, Quicksilver: 96

Fox Theatre, San Diego: 63, 64, 65

Cathe Centorbe: 167b, 194

Ben Spiegel: 193t, 193b

Palace Cultural Arts Association: 74

Ocean State Performing Arts Center: 200t

Landmark Theater Restoration: 30, 124

G. Carfora: 182

Northampton Academy of Music: 19

Robert K. Ander, Jr.: 291, 29r

Wm. Gesten, Foto Arts: 190b, 191tl

Wilmington Grand Opera House: 20

James Scherzi: 95tr

Pabst Theatre, Milwaukee: 22

Frank Dutton: 195, 196

Photographs by author: 21, 49, 50t, 50b, 51tl, 51tr, 51b, 52t, 53t, 54t, 54b, 55tl, 56t, 56b, 67, 69, 89tr, 89b, 90tr, 91b, 92, 93r, 94b, 95tr, 95b, 105bl, 107, 108, 109, 122, 146b, 147b, 149t, 149b, 150t, 150b, 151t, 151b, 152t, 152b, 173, 179, 181, 183, 185b, 187b, 188tl, 188b, 190tl, 190tr, 191tr, 191b, 192, 206, 210, 211.

**r = right,  l = left,  t = top,  b = bottom**

# ACKNOWLEDGMENTS

For providing the initial spark for the book, a standing ovation for the people who rescued the Paramount Theatre in Oakland, California, and for its chief administrators, Luana DeVol, Laura Roberts, Peter Botto, and Gene Morrison.

For my basic training I am deeply grateful to Helen Searing of Smith College, Northampton, Massachusetts and Benjamin DeMott of Amherst College, Amherst, Massachusetts.

For federal aid, my thanks to two Washingtonians: Gail Wentzell of the National Trust for Historic Preservation, for early confidence in the project, and Fifi Sheridan of the National Endowment for the Arts, for her invaluable aid at the beginning and for rooting from the stands throughout.

For extraordinary service to the cause, warm thanks to Kate Costello. For some difficult work, overdue appreciation to Rosemarie Banes and Adam Treister.

A large portion of this book would have been difficult if not impossible to produce without the help of the Theatre Historical Society, an organization formed by the late Ben Hall in 1969. In particular, I wish to acknowledge the tremendous debt owed to Brother Andrew Corsini of Notre Dame University, the archivist, editor, and heart of the organization. Among the society's other treasures are the encyclopedic memory of Joe DuciBella of Chicago and the photograph collection of Terry Helgesen. The help of these two men is deeply appreciated.

Thanks also to the following members for their insights, information, and the occasional slide: Robert K. Headley, Jr., Steve Levin, Fred Beall, Douglas Gomery, Daniel Friedman, Elliot Stein, Frank Cronican, Michael Miller, Joe Rosenberg, Bret Eddy, Jerry Alexander, William C. Frisk, Gene Chesley, Connie and Mason Bunker, David Barnett, Irv Glazer, Jamie Williams, Rick Johnson, Donald C. King, Randy Juster, John Faust, Henry Aldridge, Charles Walker, and the irrepressible Robert Foreman.

Despite the aid of all the above, this book could never have been written without the gracious cooperation of the following people, who are working to keep the surviving movie palaces in operation:

**Northeast**—Massachusetts: Duane Robinson, Northampton; Russell Durocher, Springfield; Gary Brown, Greenfield; George Miller, Pittsfield; Beth Young and Ken Townsend, Boston. Rhode Island: Robert Foreman and Marion Simon, Providence. New York: Jamie Williams, Rose Bernthal, Kim Conrad, and James Scherzi, Syracuse; Robert Kraus, Rochester; L. Curt Mangel, Buffalo; Mary Kellers, Patricia H. Robert, and the Reverends Perry and Coston, New York City. Pennsylvania: Dan Kester and Don Craig, Pittsburgh. Michigan: Thom Greene, East Lansing. Ohio: John Hemsath, Darcy Walter, Frank Dutton, and Todd Reeves, Cleveland; Randall J. Hemming, Akron; Donald R. Streibig, Mary Bishop, Jeffrey A. Frank, and Jed Ellis, Columbus; W. Alan Kirk and Julia Shelton, Marion; Larry Baker and Tom Secrist, Bellefontaine; Dotty Fitch and Linda J. Parker, Cincinnati.

**Midwest**—Illinois: John Malloy, Shirley Profeta, Danial H. Perlman, and some anonymous friends, Chicago; Peggy Tibbits, Aurora. Wisconsin: Nancy Hyndman, Jess Brownell, Mark Cooley, and Greg Stevenson, Milwaukee; Bill Metzger, Baraboo. Nebraska: Darby Hall, Omaha. Missouri: Les Pine, Kansas City; Susan Harris, St. Joseph; G. Carfora, Randy Graves, and Robert Wilkins, St. Louis.

**South**—Delaware: Michael F. Gallagher, Wilmington. Virginia: Joe Ragey, David Whitmore, and Mary Howell, Norfolk. North Carolina: John Bell and Leo Schario, Greensboro. Georgia: Alan W. McCracken and Beauchamp Carr, Atlanta. Kentucky: Shirley E. Miller, Louisville. Louisiana: Heather R. Martin, New Orleans. Florida: Carol, Dunett, Diane, Gary, Earl, and Dr. Vernita Batchelder, Tampa; Roland Wayne, Dorothy Lynch, and Arthur Brawn, Miami.

**Northwest**—Montana: Henry Lussy, Anaconda. Utah: Steve H. Horton, Salt Lake City. Colorado: Rick Wurpel and B. J. Easthay, Denver. Washington: Leon Kalimos, Richard Sanford, and Dan Quinn, Seattle.

**Southwest**—Texas: Edward Harllee, Rose Calloway, and John Richardson, San Antonio; Nancy Banister and John Bernardoni, Austin; Carol Haugh and Sam Pedigo, Dallas; Danny Miller, Abilene. New Mexico: Vincent Amendolagine and Harvey Hoshour, Albuquerque. Arizona: Walter C. Suft, Jr., Phoenix. California: George L. Gildred and Frank Vogel, Jr., San Diego; Darrel Mulvihill and Connie Majka, Catalina Island; Ave Pildas and Eli W. Tatum, Los Angeles; Suzanne Albershardt and Susan Mote, Hollywood; Sammy Zelcer, Beverly Hills; Howard Williams, Bob Tamson, and Dave Lefler, Santa Barbara; Michael Thomas and Timothy DiMasi, San Francisco; Mike Morgan, Sacramento.

**Canada**—Colin Cutts, Vancouver, British Columbia.

With apologies to forgotten friends in Detroit, Memphis, Utica, and Dubuque.

# PREFACE

No buildings in America have been, collectively, as audaciously romantic, blatantly derivative, and wonderfully original as the movie palaces. No buildings have been as loudly hyped by their owners, totally reviled by architecture critics, and well attended by local populations. The majority of these palaces were built during the years between World War I and the Great Depression. This time, the days of Gatsby and the flappers, is now fondly romanticized beyond recognition.

The years before World War I brought America a flurry of new inventions—cars, airplanes, and, most accessible of all, the movies. It took a few years for theater architects to catch up with the film makers, but once they did, their palaces frequently surpassed in flamboyant virtuosity what was shown on the silver screens. The impresario's attitude is best summed up in a line from Marcus Loew, the head of the largest movie-palace empire: "We sell tickets to theaters, not movies."

Nationwide, even the smallest towns could boast of regally outfitted movie houses, often designed by the same architects who built the big-city picture palaces. The theaters ranged in style from bewilderingly eclectic to near-perfect replicas of the finest royal palaces of Europe and the Orient. Imitation wonders of the worlds, from Mayan tombs to Babylonian hanging gardens, were incorporated into the decorative schemes. Paintings by the old masters and valuable antiques were carted to America by theater designers simply to line the walls of grand foyers

and balcony promenades. Plaster versions of the treasures of King Tut could be seen in the movie palaces long before the originals appeared in museums. The patrons were not always aware of the decorations' origins, but they flocked to see whatever spectacular arrangements the palace architects dreamed up.

What follows is the life story of these glorified structures, from the circumstances surrounding their conception to their lingering death in the age of television. There are some happy endings—or more precisely, new beginnings—to the story, as many of the old palaces have been reincarnated as homes for a variety of operations. The decorations of these new-old interiors are frequently as unusual as the original palace designs. Taking full advantage of this second chance, the proprietors of the former movie palaces have thrown open the doors once again to amaze a new generation of spectators and to stir the memories of those who can still recall the time movies cost a quarter and the theaters alone were worth the price of admission.

In 1982, New York City's Radio City Music Hall, the last of the grand-scale movie palaces to be built, will reach its fiftieth birthday. As that milestone approaches, the time has come to look back on the lost glamor of the golden age of picture palaces. We are fortunate that a sufficient number has survived to give a taste of that age. These movie houses should be prized by all as valuable ties to an age not long gone by.

# SETTING THE STAGE

# T

## THE AGE AND THE MOVIES

The origins of the movies lie within the collective genius of inventors working during the late nineteenth century. Foremost among them was Thomas Edison. Not only did Edison give the world the electric light bulb which would later illuminate the Great White Way and lend the movie palaces much of their showy glamor, but he also made valuable contributions to the birth of the movies. In 1889 he joined with film pioneer George Eastman to perfect frame-lined celluloid film, the key to putting the pictures in motion. Within three years, Edison-designed Kinetoscopes were being handcranked all across America.

The movies did not catch on with the public immmediately; they were viewed instead as a novelty. Soon, however, the potential of moving pictures to stir the emotions and present new visions was realized. The creators of the first feature-length motion picture, *The Great Train Robbery* (1903), sent trains speeding and gunfighters' bullets flying toward the camera, to the shock and delight of the first moviegoers. These were illusions that stage magicians could never hope to duplicate.

The best movies of the teens were exciting adventures and sentimental melodramas, but they lacked the vitality of post-war films. Movies first became a big business in the early 1920s, and the insatiable demand of the public for new movies was translated into more energetic comedies and swashbuckling epics.

The movies were at first primarily a reflection of contemporary life, but they came to symbolize the feverish pitch of the times and the wildest dreams of those who lived through those times. The Roaring Twenties were best captured in the films, music, and art of that period. One of the most playful visions of the era was colorfully spread across the lobby walls of the Loew's State Theater (1921) in Cleveland, Ohio. The best known of the four James Daugherty murals is titled "The Spirit of Cinema—America"; as described by a local newspaper: "The Spirit of the Cinema appears in the American tableau. Here the modern vamp supplants Helen of Troy; jazz drowns the pipes of Pan; an auto supersedes the chariot; a flying machine outsoars Pegasus; towering skyscrapers overtop the temple-crowned Acropolis; Palm Beach bathers eclipse the nymphs; the Boy Scout takes the place of the shepherd boy . . . the composition is rush hour." How better to describe the manic quality of the age?

With the advent of sound films in 1927 a new dimension was added to moviemaking. Vaudeville skits, chorus spectaculars, and ballroom acts were staged for the cameras and inserted into movies with highly romanticized plot lines to create one of film history's most famous genres, the Hollywood musical. The Depression and the Hays

Royal Theater in Kansas City, Missouri.

13

The Alhambra Theater (1927) was in a wealthy section of Sacramento. Even so, the door prize seems a bit extravagant for 1933, but the Rockne car was a lemon.

Frozen in anticipation, the crowd and attendants look to see who the next arrivals will be at the 1932 premiere of *Morocco*. The theater, Grauman's Chinese (1927), has been drawing crowds to Hollywood ever since it opened.

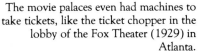

The movie palaces even had machines to take tickets, like the ticket chopper in the lobby of the Fox Theater (1929) in Atlanta.

Code (Hollywood's self-imposed censorship) robbed the movies of some of their exuberance in the mid-1930s. The response of Hollywood's screenwriters was to place their stories in the most fashionable settings, pep up the dialogue, and make the action even faster than in the musicals. As a result, dramas became more complicated and socially aware, while the comedies were more sophisticated or screwball (the best were both).

The movies also had their sober side. The newsreels gave moviegoers front-row seats for the important events of the day. While lacking the immediacy of television news, the service provided by Movietone News was no less valuable. Americans in the thirties and forties were able to witness firsthand President Roosevelt battling the Depression, the New York Yankees demolishing whatever sacrificial lamb the National League served up, and the

Allies' efforts to defeat the Axis powers.

The significance of the movie palaces to those who attended them is difficult to appreciate, especially now, when television is such a pervasive influence. More than just the primary source of entertainment, the theaters were the local gathering spots, the centers of downtown nightlife. The movies provided a release for the increasing pressures of a world growing more hectic by the day. A ticket to a show was a passport to lives and cultures otherwise beyond reach. No form of entertainment had ever been as accessible or as popular. During their peak years, the movie palaces drew full houses three or four times a day, with an extra show on weekends.

The opening of a new movie theater in town was a cause for public celebration, with all the hoopla normally reserved for a major movie premiere.

Most of the town of South Bend, Indiana showed up at the train station to greet the cast of *Knute Rockne—All American*. Pat O'Brien and Gale Page were the stars, and Ronald Reagan played a pivotal role as the Gipper.

South Bend's Colfax Theater was all decked out for the world premiere of this movie biography honoring Notre Dame's famous football coach.

And not all the movies had their gala premieres in Hollywood or New York; movies set in a specific location often opened there, no matter how small the town. The crowds would gather, the klieg lights would be set in place, and the celebrities would make their way from their limousines into the theater. No one, short of the president or Lucky Lindy, could draw a crowd as large as those that gathered for the screen idols at the big premieres.

At the heart of the matter was the power of motion pictures to touch the lives of so many. America came of age in the early part of this century but, even with the audiences' growing sophistication, the movies never lost their magic.

# ANCESTRAL ORIGINS

The movie palaces were the offsprings of a long and distinguished collection of buildings, dating back as far as the ancient Greek amphitheaters and through the formal stages of the seventeenth century. Baroque palaces, Mediterranean palazzos, Gothic cathedrals, and the temples of the Far East served to inspire the designers of the grandest movie theaters.

The buildings with the most direct bearing on shaping the movie palaces were the opera houses and music halls of the late nineteenth century. Charles Garnier's Paris Opéra (1875) stands as a suitably lavish predecessor to the movie palaces of the golden age. The monumental facade, looming over the Place de l'Opéra, epitomizes the bombastic architecture of France's Second Empire under Napoleon III. The Opera was built to be the ultimate in elegance, using only the richest materials; it remains a focus of Parisian cultural life.

Charles Garnier's grandiose design for the Paris Opéra (1875) is entirely in keeping with the building's function as a major cultural landmark.

Photo Chevoj...

Not quite so grandiose, the first movie theaters followed more closely in the architectual footsteps of the Opéra's modest American counterparts. These nineteenth-century halls, smaller in scale than the Opéra, demonstrate a sharpened sensibility toward theater construction. Whether built in the biggest city or the smallest town, these theaters were equally prized by the local citizens. The diversity of building styles popular at the time is reflected by the variety of music halls.

One of New England's best nineteenth-century halls is the Academy of Music (1891) in Northampton, Massachusetts. The theater's auditorium seats 1,040 in a cozy Victorian setting. The Academy was built by a local benefactor, H. R. Lyman, as America's first municipally owned theater. The resident theater group, the Northampton Players, gave way to movies in 1919, but not before it played host to such luminaries as Ethel Barrymore and Harry Houdini.

Architect William Brocklesby's blueprints for the Academy called for a flat brick facade along Main Street. The terra-cotta ornamental touches sprinkled liberally across the facade show classical design elements executed with a romantic Victorian sensibility. The end product was blasted by one of Brocklesby's contemporaries as a theater "of almost unbelievable exterior ugliness." Passage of time has softened this view and given the Academy of Music its picturesque charm.

Hidden by the esthetic issue is the design's unusual structural character. The function of each part of the building is clearly defined by the massing of its exterior forms. Under the stylistic banner of romantic rationalism, this approximates the "form follows function" doctrine, which has guided much of twentieth-century architecture.

Most of the nineteenth-century halls suffer in comparison with later theaters because of their characteristic squared-off look, which was necessitated by structural concerns. This short-coming was circumvented most beautifully by the inclusion of a horseshoe balcony. None curves more gracefully

*Facing page.* The height of French elegance is reflected inside the Paris Opera. This stairway served as a model for many of the movie palace architects.

The principles of nineteenth-century rationalism were put into practice by the Academy of Music (1891) in Northampton, Massachusetts. The building's classical structure came first, with the decoration layered along its surface.

The cast-iron exoskeleton of Wilmington, Delaware's Grand Opera House (1871) stands out in the night lighting.

than the golden rim of the Wilmington Grand Opera House (1871). The balcony rail decribes an elegant arc through the auditorium, relieving the boxy feeling. Spreading above the auditorium, a broad ceiling mural encircles a small, star-studded oculus. The oculus in the dome of the Pantheon in Rome was intended as a porthole to the heavens; in Wilmington it is a symbolic

gesture to the masters of trompe-l'oeil, suggesting a feeling of spaciousness possible only by illusion.

The Grand Opera House was originally designed for the Masons of Delaware by the firm of Dixon & Carson. As a result, the exterior shows a suitable civic awareness, with a rich Second Empire styling that predates the Paris Opéra. In line with much of the best

court architecture of Napoleon III, the Grand Opera House has an emphatically classical facade surmounted by a blue slate mansard roof. Unlike those of its French cousins, the Grand's exterior was not constructed in stone; instead it was given one of the finest cast-iron facades in the country. In that era, cast-iron construction was a quick and economical means of producing archi-

The bands of white stone against red brick give Cincinnati's Music Hall (1878) the look of a Victorian Gothic cathedral.

tectural ornament: sections of the facade were molded and lifted into place. The repetitious quality of this kind of ornamentation was turned to advantage at the Grand by the beautiful rhythm established with the skeletal column forms.

In sharp contrast, Cincinnati's 1878 Music Hall is Victorian Gothic in full bloom. The rose window dominat-

ing the central gable of the main facade is bracketed by pairs of towers. There is a certain heaviness to the design—a composition of 3,858,000 cherry-red bricks—by the firm of Hannaford & Proctor. This blocky quality led members of the local German population to jokingly refer to the building's style as sauerbraten-Byzantine. The huge interior is decorated in traditionally elegant

fashion, with blazes of burgundy amid cream-white colonnades trimmed in gold.

The limits of nineteenth-century technology required supporting piers for the balconies, blocking the views of at least a few patrons (cantilevering, which eliminates the needs for post support, was yet to be perfected). One method to avoid using the obstructing

The drop-off is so sharp from the top balcony of Milwaukee's Pabst Theater (1895) that not even the tall Pabst headrests block the view.

pillars was to build shallow balconies, often two or more stacked on top of each other. The cylindrical auditorium of the Pabst Theater (1895) in Milwaukee, Wisconsin, rises tall and shallow to fit in two of these shelf balconies. The rich decoration, commonly labeled German baroque, creates intimacy rather than confinement. Those making the trip to the top balcony are rewarded with a seat in one of the original high-back chairs, the Pabst name worked into the grillwork head supports. Ornate lattice-work outlines the tall proscenium arch, above which a bronzed (if not bronze) Apollo raises his lyre. The overall composition is the work of Otto Strack, the architect of the Pabst breweries.

An important landmark in the history of modern architecture, Dankmar Adler and Louis Sullivan's Auditorium Building in Chicago is the most pertinent among the nineteenth-century buildings to the development of the movie palaces. Designed to house several facilities under its roof, the Auditorium Building was the city's tallest structure at its completion. In addition to the beautifully appointed Auditorium Theatre (1889), the building originally contained a hotel, bar, and a number of offices, including the architect's own in the tower above the Congress Avenue facade. The finishing touches, on top of the tower, were an

Adler & Sullivan's Auditorium Building played an important role in Chicago's rise to architectural pre-eminence. The functional wonders of the Auditorium Theatre (1889) made it America's first modern theater.

observatory and weather-station.

The rusticated stonework of the building's exterior gives way inside to Sullivan's intricate ornamentation. The Auditorium Theatre, the building's centerpiece, is a marvel in its structural properties as well as its decorative ones. The one feature of the Auditorium most significant to the movie palaces is its double-shell construction. A plaster shell is suspended inside the girded box of the auditorium frame. Adler's radiating arches, each coated with Sullivan's pale gold handiwork, possess no structural value, but they hold the secret of the Auditorium's famed acoustics. The flattened modeling and surface detail of the arches combine to give the auditorium the ideal shape for perfect sound, providing a resonant surface while masking unwelcome echoes.

Great foresight is revealed in the manner in which Adler & Sullivan incorporated the Auditorium's mechanical services into its architecture. Strung along the arches is an ingenious, fully integrated lighting system, one of the first in the country. Alternating with Sullivan's light fixtures are his "gilded beehive" hemispheres, which serve as ventilation ducts. The Auditorium even had primitive air conditioning in summer; huge blocks of ice were placed in the ventilation shafts.

Other technical innovations include the eleven hydraulic stage lifts, the portable stage apron for covering the orchestra pit, and the reducing curtain. This curtain is actually three bronze panels that define the stage opening; the side panels are raised or lowered to change its width. At the rear of the auditorium, hinged panels swing down to close off the gallery and upper balcony sections. The Auditorium Theatre originally seated 4,237 on four levels; thirty years elapsed before a movie theater of equal size was built.

Cast ornament covered the flat exterior of Baltimore's Pickwick, *above*. The box office was a small art nouveau masterpiece.

A carnival atmosphere was suggested by the stud-lighted and arched exterior of the Saxe Theater, *right*, in Minneapolis.

# VAUDEVILLE HOUSES AND NICKELODEONS

The palaces' nearest relatives, in time if not style, were the nickelodeons and vaudeville houses built just after the turn of the century. Art nouveau was then in vogue in America, as evidenced by much of theater design of that period. Art nouveau had its origins in the arts and crafts movement of mid-nineteenth-century England, with its celebration of hand-wrought decoration over the early intimations of mass-produced architecture. The practition-

ers of art nouveau relaxed the stance against machine-aided ornaments, as long as they appeared sufficiently naturalistic and organic.

Art nouveau flourishes were visible in the facades of many nickelodeons. The oversized terra-cotta decorations of these richly designed fronts were often ordered from catalogs of manufactured ornaments provided by the Decorator Supply Company of Chicago or one of their competitors.

Nearly all the decoration went on the outside. Most of the nickelodeons were small, family-operated businesses, located in simple storefronts. Among these was the first building devoted exclusively to showing movies, a Pittsburgh shop built in 1905. The rising popularity of motion pictures made the small size of these storefront theaters a problem. The Dreamland (1907) in Portland, Maine, was closed after only two years of operation when the own-

Chicago's Bijou Dream featured a glass staircase above a cascading stream of water lighted in different colors. A ticket to the main floor cost a dime, but for a nickel you got a trip up that magical staircase and a seat in the balcony.

New England's first movie house was the Dreamland Theatre (1907) in Portland, Maine.

ers realized they needed a larger theater.

The vaudeville houses were larger, a fact that did not escape the notice of some smart film exhibitors. The big break for the movies came when they gained second billing in these halls, behind the popular stage acts of the day. As motion pictures grew in both audience appeal and technical quality, they eventually took over the top spot in the act as well as the old vaudeville halls.

The best survivors among these amusement halls show their age by touches of art nouveau ornamentation.

The New Amsterdam Theatre (1903) on New York City's Forty-second Street is one of the purest examples of art nouveau in the country. The rich, romantic styling spreads throughout the theater. The outer lobby contains a set of bronze doors, elegantly cast in relief, worthy of Charles Rennie Mackintosh, the great Scottish art nouveau architect. Set above the doors are ivory-colored bas-relief panels depicting scenes from Shakespeare (behind one of these doors Florenz Ziegfeld discovered Irene Dunne and started her on the way to film stardom). The stair-

cases to the balconies are decorated with a mass of sinuous art nouveau detail: sculpted faces are camouflaged by the woven vines of the newel posts, and vegetal patterns are carried up along the bannisters.

The predominant themes of nature and drama continued in the New Amsterdam's auditorium, particularly in the allegorical scenes portrayed above the proscenium arch and boxes. The proscenium opening is outlined by sixteen dark green peacocks sculpted into the plasterwork. Each of the deep, saucer-shaped boxes, stag-

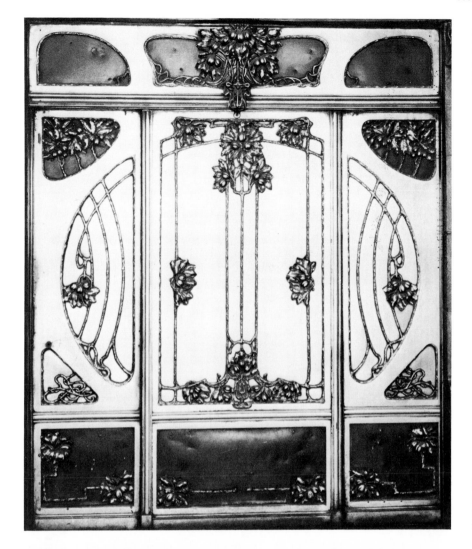

*Facing page.* Silent film star John Bunny had this theater named in his honor. The theater, in the Washington Heights section of Manhattan, still operates as the Nova Theater.

The art nouveau character of the New Amsterdam (1903) in New York extends to the exquisitely patterned elevator doors in the outer lobby.

There is hardly a straight line or flat surface to be found in the auditorium of the New Amsterdam.

The 1925 *Follies* was Florenz Ziegfeld's tenth production at the New Amsterdam. The carved figures above the canopy marquee were removed when a streamlined vertical marquee was installed in the 1930s.

gered six to a side, was styled to represent a flower, after which the box was named (the boxes have been removed). The chairs in these boxes, as well as those in the various lobbies and lounges, were constructed from handcarved wooden pieces, fashioned in a variety of art nouveau patterns. The New Amsterdam also boasts New York's first cantilever arch-supported balcony. The balcony and the decoration were the work of Herts & Tallant, the firm that later designed the Brooklyn Academy of Music (1908).

Before the New Amsterdam began showing movies in 1937, it was home for fifteen years to some prominent stage productions. Flo Ziegfeld staged his *Follies* in the auditorium of the New Amsterdam from 1913 through 1927. The popularity of the *Follies* led Ziegfeld to introduce a second show, the *Frolics*, on top of the New Amsterdam Building. Roof theaters were frequently included in the theater designs of the period as a way of circumventing the weather problems that plagued enclosed theaters in summer. With his trademark flamboyance, Ziegfeld and the *Frolics* turned the New Amsterdam's Roof Theatre into one of the hottest, and coolest, nightspots in the city.

The Boston Majestic (1903, now the Saxon) was built the same year as the New Amsterdam, but architect

After the exuberance of art nouveau, the graceful side-wall ornament of Norfolk's Wells Theatre (1913) seems almost bare.

The exterior of the Wells is essentially a Renaissance palazzo executed in brick. Cast-iron ornaments trim the canopy marquee.

John Galen Howard put a classical mask over an auditorium that retains a few art nouveau touches. While the front facade is flatly classical with some low-relief floral ornamentation, the interior design is somewhat looser, with a gracefully rounded auditorium ceiling. A row of winged angels grows out of the side walls to support the upper balcony.

Ten years after the New Amsterdam was completed, art nouveau had

given way completely to Beaux-Arts classicism, a much more formal style with fewer ornamental touches. The Wells Theatre (1913) in Norfolk, Virginia, originally a vaudeville house, was one of the last theaters built before the movies gained their independence. Aside from a few more load-bearing angels at the rear of the main floor, ornamentation and spatial arrangement inside the Wells are entirely in keeping with the ideals of contained opulence

that prevailed during the Beaux-Arts period. The traditional tiers of boxes line the auditorium walls in descending rows. The exterior is an attractive rendition of a Renaissance palazzo. This is the sort of treatment found in the architecture of the first movie theaters, then making their entrance.

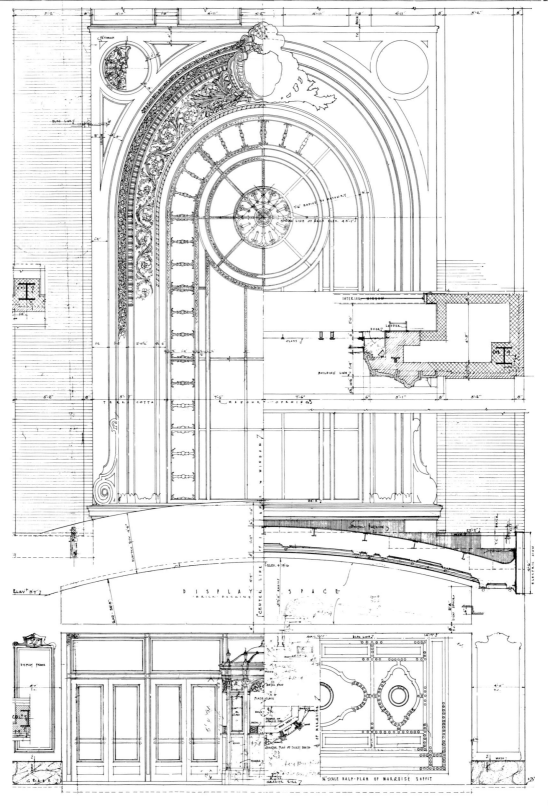

SET No.

OFFICE OF
THO$. W. LAMB
ARCHITECT
NEW YORK CITY

# THE PALACE ARCHITECTS

2

## A MATTER OF TASTE

A certain suspension of adherence to standard architectural doctrines is required before one can properly evaluate the movie palaces and their position in the history of the art of building. Questions of stylistic integrity—and of simple good taste—have plagued the movie theaters since their birth. Architectural classification is no easy matter; the movie palaces either defy specific stylistic labels or demand a number of these labels strung together. As palace historian Ben Hall wrote in *The Best Remaining Seats*, "the architecture of the movie palace was a triumph of suppressed desire, and its practitioners ranged in style from the purely classic to a wildly abandoned eclectic."

The latter characteristic, a freestyle approach to design, drew the wrath of architecture critics over the years. Thomas E. Tallmadge, a contemporary of the palace architects, voiced his complaint in a 1928 issue of *Motion Picture News*: "No more pitiful degradation of an art has ever been presented than the prostitution of architecture that goes on daily in the construction of these huge buildings . . . taste and beauty abased to the lowest degree."

The theater builders saw their role in a different light. Their purpose was to build a showplace with all the trappings of the rich, but accessible to all. George Rapp, a leading palace architect, put it best: "Here is a shrine to democracy where the wealthy rub elbows with the poor."

This kind of thinking lent the movie theaters a mass appeal which had been absent in the grand opera houses of the previous era. *American Theaters of Today* published an interview in 1929 with palace decorator Harold Rambusch in which he traced further the populist reasoning behind the theaters: "No kings or emperors have ever wandered through more luxurious surroundings. In a sense, those theaters are a social safety valve in that the public can partake of the same luxuries as the rich, and use them to the same full extent."

This philosophy irritated social critics nearly as much as it did architecture critics. In 1927 Rabindranath Tagore, writing for the *Atlantic Monthly*, spoke out against the kind of undiluted democracy symbolized by the movie palaces: "It makes a deliberate study of the dark patches of the human intellect wherewith to help create an atmosphere of delusion through hints, gestures, yells, and startling grimaces for the purpose of stupefying the public mind." The single exception Tagore made was for the austere Eastman Theater (1921) in Rochester, New York. The theater, a pet project of George Eastman, was designed by McKim, Mead & White more as a traditional orchestra hall than a movie palace. The Eastman Theater certainly re-

Blueprint from the office of Thomas W. Lamb for the Loew's State Theater (1928) in Syracuse, New York.

sembles a nineteenth-century European concert hall, with an interior of restrained elegance in a staid Beaux-Arts box.

In contrast, the palace architects were undoubtedly guilty of excess ornamentation, all of it flagrantly derivative. The designers of the movie palaces drew their inspiration from architectural style books, which contained measured patterns for the ornamental elements of every age and culture. The palace architects were not alone in borrowing from the past; the art-historical approach flourished in America for the first quarter of the twentieth century. The builders of libraries, railway stations, government offices, and private homes all utilized the ornaments of other eras to beautify their structures. Style books were an essential part of every architect's library.

Within a decade after the close of the golden age in the early 1930s, the architectural leadership had turned its back on recipe-book design. During the heyday of the palaces, the principles of the International style, largely responsible for shaping our present-day cities, were being formulated in Europe. The founders of what became known as the modern style viewed applied ornament as a crime, accepting only whatever esthetic value could be incorporated within the structure and materials. For these architect theorists, the movie palaces would naturally be anathema. Writing in 1940, as the International style was reaching its peak, critic Talbot Hamlin blasted such eclecticism: "The faded reworking of old themes in twentieth-century eclectic architecture had become a meaningless amusement of dilettante architects and clients who had substituted canons of arbitrary, learned-by-rote taste for any sense of creative design, and had reduced architecture to the level of mere window dressing."

Such a mass indictment touches least upon the palace architects. The fantastic nature of their buildings should give them a certain immunity from stylistic criticism. Rather than censured, these architects should have been congratulated for creating some of the most spectacularly romantic interiors ever conceived.

Ultimately it was all part of the show. It is not surprising that talented architects were brought in to design the opulent movie showplaces. The palaces were major commissions, built for millions of pre-Depression dollars. At worst the palace architects can be accused of catering to mass taste. Certainly the moviegoing public was delighted by these regally outfitted imitations of the grandest Old World halls and palaces. The air of sophistication and high culture associated with the solidly established styles attracted the public, and this the palace architects provided in abundance.

# THE BUILDING PROGRAM

Aside from the skyscraper, no building type is more clearly representative of twentieth-century American architecture than the movie palace. The palace architects were faced with a building program almost unrivaled in their day in complexity, requiring a vast collection of rooms under one roof and often situated on ridiculously irregular plots of land. British architect Clifford Worthington wrote in 1931, "Of all buildings, none are more fascinating to design, nor more difficult to construct than the cinema." Nonetheless, the movie palaces went up all around the country, often at breakneck speed. During the peak construction years, 1925 through 1930, even the largest theaters were usually completed in well under a year, although the workmen may not have tacked down the last piece of carpet until a few minutes before the opening.

Built decades before Hollywood created the motion-picture extravaganza, the theaters were spectacles in their own right. The movie palaces were built not just to express the romantic extremes of architectural design, but also to serve a purpose purely economic in nature; to draw patrons to the box office.

The exteriors of the movie palaces helped to fulfill this end. While rarely as opulent or exotic as the interiors, the facades were still quite distinct from the surrounding cityscape. Even if the theater were housed within an office block it could be distinguished by its broad canopy marquee, often supplemented by a towering vertical marquee. The theater designers pioneered the use of electric lighting as advertisement. Their special effects included tracer and chaser light bulbs and rows of stud lights used to outline the ornamental shapes of the facades. More glitter was provided for the grand theater openings and movie premieres, which required blazing klieg lights to illuminate the night skies and to spotlight the famous stars in attendance. During quieter times, oversize promotional pictures around the deluxe box offices helped draw the crowds.

Once through the bronze outer doors of a movie palace, the ticket holder inevitably found himself progressing through a breathtaking group of lobby spaces. Sometimes the lobbies

A pair of construction shots of the Loew's United Artists (1928) in Louisville, Kentucky, presents a clear model of standard palace architecture. In the early view, the steel framework outlines the stage housing, the sharp slope of the balcony (in contrast to the shallow rake of the main floor), and the roof covering, from which the auditorium's plaster ceiling was hung on heavy strands of cable.

Stud lighting gave Chicago's Marbro Theater (1927) the appearance of a huge wedding cake.

This promotional stunt, staged in 1935 in front of the Loew's State (1926) on New Orleans's Canal Street, shows the lengths (or heights) to which the owners would go to attract customers.

Rising a full ten stories along the side of the Michigan Theater (1926) in Detroit, this must have been the most awesome vertical marquee ever built.

The outer lobby of the Rialto Square Theater (1926) in Joliet, Illinois, is almost absurdly grand. Could any movie match such a spectacle?

were more impressive than the auditorium. Put simply, by designer E. C. A. Bullock of the firm of Rapp & Rapp, the lobbies had to be spectacular "to keep the patron's mind off the fact that he is waiting." Leading off these lobbies were promenades filled with expensive art objects and magnificent staircases.

With several shows a day instead of a single play or concert, easing the flow of patrons in and out of the theater became a prime consideration. The palace architects carefully worked out crowd circulation patterns to insure safety and convenience. The Tivoli Theater in Chicago, designed by Rapp & Rapp in 1921, was the first movie theater with a clearly charted traffic pattern. The architects were aided in their efforts by a feature they did not have to design, for the flow of people was directed by the movie palace's own brand of traffic cop, the usher. The elite corps of ushers was uniformed and trained like a crack drill unit. At the Saenger Theater in New Orleans, the 100 members of the palace guard were known collectively as "The Soldiers of Service." The position of usher carried great honor and serious responsibility.

The ushers directed patrons to more parts of the theater than the seats. The ornate lobbies and auditoriums were the most magnificent areas of any movie palace, but there were other public spaces provided for the patrons' convenience. Small children could be taken to specially designed playrooms, where the theater's resident nurse would carefully supervise them during the show. Exotic lounges were included for smoking or just sitting. Furniture

The children's playroom in the Chicago Paradise (1928) allowed parents to see a movie and save the price of a babysitter.

The Paramount (1931) in Aurora, Illinois, *bottom left*, never had a playroom. Instead, the owners took advantage of an empty lot next to the theater and created Paramount Park.

from royal mansions sometimes found its way into the men's and women's lounges.

The backstage rooms were nearly as diverse in their functions as the public rooms. Actors' dressing rooms were stacked up at either end of the stage and additional dressing rooms were provided below stage for the theater musicians who played during the live part of the show. Top-flight orchestras of the day filled the pits of the palaces, playing everything from classical masterpieces to contemporary hits. Competition among theaters for well-known conductors was fierce; it was rumored that the 1926 Oriental Theater in Chicago was built just to showcase Paul Ash and

A cultural safari by Anne Dornan, chief designer of Loew's Ohio (1928) in Columbus, resulted in the Africa Room. The decor of this lower lounge has no relation to the overall style of the theater.

When the Vanderbilts' Manhattan townhouse was demolished in the midtwenties, the Loew's Corporation managed to salvage a considerable portion of the interior. The Vanderbilt's Oriental Room was transported in pieces to Kansas City, Missouri, where it was reassembled as a women's lounge in the Loew's Midland Theater (1927).

Many movie palaces had pianos on the mezzanines to keep waiting patrons entertained, but the Music Room of the San Francisco Fox (1929), *below*, was the only mezzanine with its own organ.

The most famous organs of the golden age were the mighty Wurlitzers, but the era's greatest showman, Samuel L. "Roxy" Rothapfel, commissioned the Kimball Organ Company to build the three five-manual organs for his Roxy Theatre (1927), *above*, in New York.

his band. Entire rooms were given over to holding the orchestra's sheet music. The music library of the Detroit Fox remains intact to this day, its value appraised at $500,000.

As any moviegoer of the silent era could attest, the orchestra members were not the only musicians in the theater. The house organists were true celebrities. The best of them added immeasurably to the enjoyment of a movie by their dexterous accompaniment. The organs also received star treatment, rising majestically from their pits, the number of manuals and ranks proudly trumpeted in the advertising literature. These instruments could lit-

Patrons never got to see the machinery that kept the theaters in operation. Nevertheless, the rooms of pipes, fans, and other equipment were kept as clean as the theaters' public areas. (Loew's United Artists, Louisville)

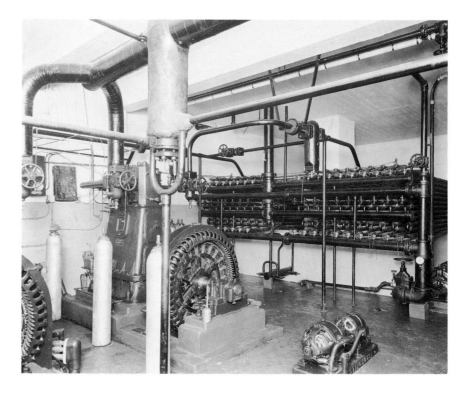

erally rock the house. Their power lay in chambers out of public view, in room after room of pipes stacked behind ornamental organ screens.

Tucked beneath the collection of public and performing spaces was the sprawling subterranean area needed to house the theater's support system. Huge machines were needed to heat and ventilate these buildings. The methods the palace architects devised for cooling such tremendous volumes of space played an important role in the development of modern air-conditioning systems. Early breakthroughs in theater cooling by Rapp & Rapp gave their clients near total domination of Chicago's market for movies in the summer, when most theaters were forced to close.

The electrical plants were also major operations. In that era of energy spendthrifts, one Chicago designer boasted that the Orpheum Theater (built in 1926 as the Palace), housed within the Metropolitan office block, would have a vertical marquee that "will burn more current by fifty per cent than the entire 22-story office building."

All this just to see a movie. The nickelodeon was left far behind.

# THE FIRST PALACES

The 1913 Regent Theater, just north of Central Park in Manhattan, is generally acknowledged to be the first deluxe theater built expressly for showing movies. The facade is a modest relative of Venice's Palace of the Doges, executed in white terra-cotta with green accents. The symmetrical colonnade enclosing the arched entryway is echoed in the twin loggia at the upper corners of the facade. The interior is traditional in ornament and spatial organization, still nineteenth-century in character. The theater still stands—a miracle considering how little remains from New York City's early romance with the movie palace.

The place of the Regent in movie-palace history is assured by its architect, Thomas W. Lamb, and its first business manager, Samuel L. Rothapfel.

Lamb had designed only one theater before the Regent, the 1910 City Photoplays, for exhibitor William Fox. Several hundred commissions were to follow.

Struggling to compete with nearby vaudeville houses, the Regent's owners brought in Rothapfel (later Rothafel) from the Midwest to rescue them. Some major innovations by the man the world would come to know as Roxy included putting the orchestra on stage, framing the movie screen with an ornate stage set, and moving the projector down to orchestra level to improve the quality of the picture. At the end of its first year, the Regent's business was

good, but Roxy's sights were set on Broadway.

The Orpheum Theater (now the Capitol) in Salt Lake City, Utah was built in the same year as the Regent and possesses a similarly Italianate main facade. G. Albert Lansburgh designed the Orpheum as a vaudeville house; it remained so until the Vitaphone sound system introduced the area to talkies in 1929, with a showing of the Warner Brothers' feature *On Trial*. A general remodeling of the auditorium gave the theater the scale, if not the feel, of a twenties movie palace.

Outstanding among early West Coast movie houses were the T & D

(1915, razed) in Oakland, California, and Seattle's Coliseum (1916). Cunningham & Politeo's design for the T & D lagged behind stylistically in its blend of art nouveau and Beaux-Arts elements. The facade was particularly unusual, with skeletal art nouveau fenestration. In contrast, the Coliseum's monumental exterior shows a neoclassical bent, typical of most of the thea-

Vaudeville was on the way out when this photograph was taken (1926), but it was still part of the show at the Regent (1913), New York City's first big movie theater.

The vertical marquee and special lighting help distinguish Seattle's Coliseum Theater (1916), *above*, from the major public buildings of the day, which share the theater's classical features.

The Second Empire style of nineteenth-century France resurfaced in 1910 at the center of Dubuque, Iowa, decorating the front of the Majestic (now the Five Flags), *right*.

ters built over the next decade by B. Marcus Priteca, the Coliseum's architect.

While each of these early movie theaters has its special qualities, none is quite so palatial as the Al Ringling Memorial Theater (1915) in Baraboo, Wisconsin—"Circus City." The famous "Master Showman of the Big Tops" wanted a unique movie house for the town that was his circus's winter home. Ringling gave the commission to Rapp & Rapp, whose first independent work had been Dubuque's Majestic Theater (1910, now the Five Flags). That theater's solid, French-opera-house exterior encloses a stack of ornate, curving balconies in the manner of Milwaukee's Pabst Theater.

For the Baraboo theater, Rapp & Rapp took a fairly plain theater plan they had executed in 1914 in Champaign, Illinois for the Orpheum, added the glories of prerevolutionary France, and gave Ringling a true palace. An elliptical ring of golden Corinthian columns outlines an auditorium designed after La Salle de Spectacle, the opera hall at Versailles. Seventeen boxes were set between the columns, and murals of angels and cherubs in delicate pastel shades were above them. The lone exception was the panel above Al Ringling's private box at the rear of the auditorium. Legend has it that he was superstitious about dead children and had the mural above his box repainted without the cherubs. Alas, Ringling himself was dead two months after the theater opened.

Breaking with the French theme of the auditorium, the lobby design owes more to Italy. The decorative frieze that rings the elliptical lobby is a copy, at one-third the scale, of the choir gallery of the sacristy in the cathedral of Florence, executed in 1671 by Luca della Robbia. In the Ringling, the sculpted fruits and bouquets blend perfectly with the ceiling mural. The artistry here and in the auditorium was that of European craftsmen who had originally come to America to work on the 1900 World's Fair and then settled in Chicago. Rapp & Rapp tapped this resource many times in the years to come.

The arched entryway of the Al Ringling Memorial Theater (1915) in Baraboo, Wisconsin, recalls standard nickelodeon fronts. The palatial portion is contained within.

The tiny rotunda lobby of the Ringling Memorial as it originally appeared—the mural and the frieze remain in good condition, but a candy counter has replaced the marble fountain.

# BROADWAY, THE LOOP, AND BEYOND

As the market for the movies grew, would-be impresarios in the big cities began pouring money into movie-theater construction. The economics of film exhibition made multiple theater operations the logical path to success, and major theater chains spread quickly to take advantage of the movie boom. It was just a short step from movie chains to the studio system; the film exhibitors aligned themselves with the Hollywood film makers as a means of providing their theaters with quality pictures (and crushing competion). Their collaboration was effective throughout the Depression and war years, and in 1948 government trust-busters moved in to break up the party.

When the studio chains were forming in the early 1920s, the commissions for their theaters naturally went to the architects who had built the first movie palaces in the big cities. In New York the top talent was Thomas Lamb. Following his success with the Regent Theater, Lamb brought his expertise to Broadway. He dotted the Great White Way with the Strand (1914, razed), the Rialto (1916, razed), and the Parthenon-faced Rivoli (1917). Master showman Roxy, making his own climb to the top, followed right behind Lamb, insuring the success of each new theater.

Lamb ended his Broadway run in 1919, building the Capitol Theater (razed) with an unprecedented 5,000-plus seating capacity. A businesslike classical facade concealed one of the most opulent interiors of Lamb's early work. The sweeping marble staircase, crystal chandeliers, and massive, dark, fluted columns of the grand foyer gave way to a huge auditorium, its great dome covered by a delicate silver bas-relief. Built for another domineering impresario, Major Bowes, the Capitol nonetheless had Roxy for its master of ceremonies. The theater was the site of Roxy's first live radio broadcasts in

1922. At the beginning of his radio career Roxy contented himself with simply airing the music and describing the acts on stage at the Capitol. Eventually he decided to produce shows in a studio solely for radio broadcast. These entertainment shows were the first of their kind. (Roxy's broadcasts had their humanitarian side; he began a widely hailed campaign to supply radios to hospitalized war veterans.) Radio made Roxy nationally famous, but his first love remained the movie palaces.

In these early Broadway movie theaters Thomas Lamb developed the style of theater design that was his trademark for much of his career. The interiors of the early showplaces reflected Lamb's fondness for the decorative classical treatment popularized in eighteenth-century Great Britain by fellow Scotsman Robert Adam. In the manner of Adam, Lamb softened formal classicism by coating nearly every surface with delicate floral bas-relief. Lamb's Adamesque period found its first clear expression in the Loew's Palace (1918, razed) in Washington, D.C. Adamesque design remained Lamb's preferred treatment through the early twenties, when he worked for three theater chains.

Lamb sprinkled New England with Adam-inspired Poli Palaces for impresario Sylvester Zefferino Poli. Poli had arrived in New York City from Italy in 1881 to work as a wax-figure modeler for the Eden Musée, a popular nineteenth-century wax museum. In the early 1890s Poli's interests shifted to vaudeville. By 1895 he had his first theater, a 2,000-seat house in New Haven, Connecticut. By the time Poli hired Thomas Lamb to refurbish the Poli Palace (1922) in Waterbury, Connecticut, Poli had a string of theaters. Lamb not only built theaters for the chain, but also remodeled most of Poli's other theaters along Adamesque lines.

Lamb designed a few theaters for the Proctor vaudeville circuit in Manhattan and upstate New York. Before the end of the twenties, both the Proctor and the Poli chains were swallowed up by larger organizations. Control of Proctor went to the RKO chain in 1929. RKO (Radio Keith Orpheum) had been formed just two years earlier, when the new giant Radio Corporation of America (RCA) took over the venerable Keith-Albee-Orpheum vaudeville circuit. Such moves hastened the death of vaudeville; live acts now reached their audiences by radio and the big palaces were abandoned to the movies. Vaudeville in New England was finished when S. Z. Poli's operation was absorbed into the Loew's chain of movie houses.

Lamb's most important business relationship was formed with Marcus Loew. Loew's theater empire eventually covered half the country, and Lamb designed the majority of the chain's theaters.

One predominant motif in Lamb's theaters was the treatment of the opera boxes, which were grouped along the side walls, and slung between sets of engaged columns. Lamb used this composition for theaters as late as the Loew's State (1924) in St. Louis and the Proctor's (1926) in Schenectady, New York. The last Adamesque side boxes, for the Proctor's 86th Street Theater in New York (1927, razed), were perhaps Lamb's best, set in near perfect harmony wth the column arrangement. Above the auditoriums, Lamb favored the use of flattened domes. Their surfaces enriched by bas-relief ornamental patterns in concentric rings out to the rim.

Another highlight of this period was his magnificent lobby design. Two of the grandest of the grand lobbies were side by side in Cleveland, in Marcus Loew's Ohio and State Theaters (both 1921). The origin of Lamb's

The side wall treatment found in the Loew's State (1924) in St. Louis is typical of how Thomas Lamb designed nearly all his theaters in the early twenties.

The original appointments of the mezzanine lobby were indisputably regal inside the Poli Palace (1926) in Worcester, Massachusetts.

design appears to be the opulent gallery of Francis I in the sixteenth-century palace at Fontainebleau. The lobbies resemble that gallery in their decorative patterns as well as in their grandeur, with walnut wainscoting surmounted by a rich mixture of large murals and smaller paintings. Among Lamb's Poli theaters, the mezzanine lobby of the Palace (1926) in Worcester, Massachusetts, possessed a stately beauty that few of Lamb's contemporaries could match.

Among the architects who ranked with Lamb were George and C. W. Rapp, the designers of the Al Ringling Memorial in Baraboo, Wisconsin. The lack of a single Loew's theater in Chicago is evidence of the near-total domination of that city's theater exhibition by the team of A. J. Balaban and Sam Katz. To design their movie-palace empire, B & K (as Chicagoans knew them) went directly to Rapp & Rapp. As a latter-day Rapp,

The great arched facade of the Chicago Theater (1921) dominates the north end of State Street in Chicago's Loop district.

grandnephew C. W. Rapp, noted, "The Rapps delivered what the Balabans wanted in theaters—a grand plan executed with taste."

Following construction of the Central Park (1917, razed) and the Riviera (1919), two handsome trial runs away from the downtown Loop, the firm was commissioned to design Chicago's first big movie palaces. Most prominent among them was the Chicago Theater (1921), the flagship of the B & K chain. Fronting on State Street, the Chicago announces its design theme by its stud-lighted Arc de Triomphe facade. Inside and out, the Chicago is pure French, like a Ringling Memorial of palatial proportions. The

Foremost among the trailblazing design features of the Chicago Theater was the use of decorative organ screens in place of traditional side boxes.

scale of the Chicago was something wholly new for movie theaters in the Midwest. The theater in Baraboo was fit for royalty, but the Chicago Theater matched the finery, with 3,880 seats to the Ringling Memorial's 804. The special charm of the Chicago Theater derives from the surprising sense of intimacy possible even in the last rows of the balcony. The reason for this is the shape of the auditorium, which is wider

The owners of the larger theaters often had difficulty coaxing patrons to make the long climb to the balcony seats. The twisting grand staircase in the Chicago Theater is a powerful incentive.

*Facing page.* Louis Sullivan's stencil designs decorate the opera boxes of the Auditorium Theatre (1889) in Chicago.

than it is deep. Spanning 170 feet, a one-piece girder supports the 68-ton balcony. The murals that line the edge of the ceiling look back to Baraboo, but the decorative organ screens, characteristic of most later movie palaces, had replaced the Ringling's side boxes. Above the auditorium, a recessed dome is punctured by a ring of bull's-eye openings illuminated by hidden cove lighting in a range of colors.

For patrons awaiting entry to this regal auditorium, further delights were present. The grand lobby, lined by a row of tall marble columns, rivals the great hall of the Paris Opéra for formal grandeur. At one end of the lobby a broad, curving grand staircase leading to the mezzanine and balcony weaves in and out of view.

As beautiful as the Chicago's grand lobby is, it was no match for the foyer of the Tivoli (1921, razed), another French jewel which Rapp & Rapp set in south Chicago. The high point of the Tivoli, opened a few months before the Chicago, was the great hall of Corinthian columns, an arrangement the firm used many times in later theaters. More Rapp & Rapp Versailles, the foyer was modeled after the Chapelle Royale, designed by Mansart for Louis XIV in

1710 and labeled by Voltaire "a gigantic piece of costume jewelry." Whatever its merits as a chapel, it made quite a lobby.

To the north of the Loop, Rapp & Rapp covered an entire block with the Uptown (1925). Here they departed completely, for perhaps the only time, from their preferred Sun King style—there is not a hint of Versailles in the theater. The decor inside and out is mainly Spanish Renaissance.

The ornamental terra-cotta facade rises as tall as an eight-story building. The marquee for the opening boasted of "an acre of seats in a magic city . . . a

The Chicago Auditorium Theatre's pale gold arches, *right*—Adler & Sullivan's perfect blend of acoustics and esthetics.

A golden horseshoe balcony, *below*, cuts through the interior of the Grand Opera House (1871) in Wilmington, Delaware.

Decorative support in Boston; a winged angel carries the balcony inside the Saxon Theater (1903), *top left*, and a cherubic face peers out from the base of a column along the side wall of the Savoy (1928, formerly Keith's Memorial), *top right*.

Movies quickly gave way to symphonic performances inside McKim, Mead & White's Eastman Theater (1921), *left*, in Rochester, New York.

Rapp & Rapp's favorite foyer treatment, borrowed from the Chapelle Royale at Versailles, was first used in the Tivoli Theater (1921) in Chicago.

Lafayette's featured role on the asbestos curtain reflects the predominant French theme of the Al Ringling Memorial Theatre (1915), the showplace of Baraboo, Wisconsin.

The cove lighting nearly overpowers the decoration above the auditorium of the Chicago Theater (1921), *above*.

Even the rear wall of the Chicago Theater's auditorium, *left*, was beautifully designed in Rapp & Rapp's French palatial.

Gusman Center (1926, formerly the Olympia), *right*, in Miami is lighted in the bright color combinations typical of John Eberson's atmospheric theaters.

A dark night sky above the courtyard walls of the Tampa Theater (1926), *below*, another of John Eberson's Florida atmospherics.

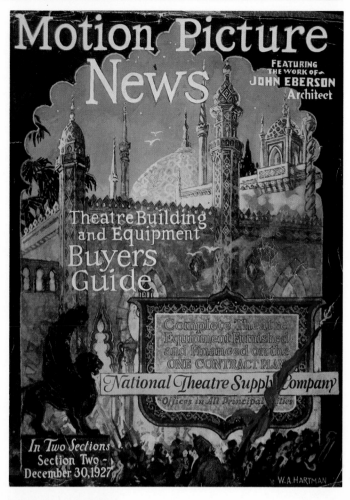

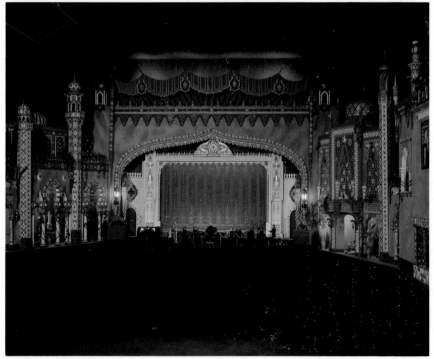

Inside the Loew's Akron (1929), *top left*, an organ screen juts into the orchestra like a ship's prow.

The Middle Eastern spirit of Chicago's Avalon Theater (1927) was captured by this rendering, *top right*, done for a *Motion Picture News* cover story on John Eberson and his atmospheric theaters.

A remarkably faithful re-creation of the Avalon's interior, *left*, fills a ten-foot-high basement in Flushing, New York.

A pair of lobby fountains: Neptune spouting in the basement of New Orleans's Saenger Theater (1927) and a polychrome tile creation in the Keith's (1928) in Flushing, New York, one of Thomas Lamb's few atmospheric theaters.

The stage ornaments of Chicago's Tivoli Theater (1921), like those of the Chicago, had to be modified to accommodate a wider screen and bigger stage acts. The cut-in orchestra was a casualty of these changes.

*Facing page.* Rapp & Rapp opted for Spanish over French only once—but on a huge scale, as can be judged from the grand foyer of Chicago's Uptown Theater (1925).

The spacious auditorium of the Uptown rises out of the picture, with only the second of the three dome basins visible.

The immenseness of the Uptown, *below,* is inescapable even underneath the balcony.

palace of enchantment in Old Spain.'' The towering lobbies resemble nothing so much as a string of overdecorated railroad concourses laid end to end. The Uptown's auditorium is even more imposing. It seats 4,325, hundreds more than any other Rapp & Rapp theater. (Its 46,000-square-foot main floor was unsurpassed until Radio City Music Hall was built seven years later.) The auditorium ceiling is a set of three inverted basins, one inside another. To brighten this spectacle, Rapp & Rapp included a colossal lighting board, with a different color for every part of the show.

The Rapps' connection with B & K ultimately took them beyond Chicago. Barney Balaban, A. J. 's brother, set out to become a film mogul by joining with Adolph Zukor's Famous Players-Lasky Corporation to form the Paramount-Publix chain. As president of Paramount, Barney directed most of the chain's commissions to Rapp & Rapp. In 1928 Rapp & Rapp became Paramount's ambassadors to the Northwest, designing the chain's outposts in Seattle and Portland. By the end of the decade even New Yorkers could sample the glories of royal France, Rapp & Rapp style.

# THE OLD GUARD

In various parts of the country, the studio chains hired local architects to design movie palaces of the same quality as those in Chicago and New York. Accordingly, most of the theaters in the early twenties were designed along the lines of the established styles.

Most traditional among the palace architects was the firm of Hoffman & Henon. The firm's design theory can best be seen in the words of its president, Paul J. Henon, writing in 1928: "Once the movies grew to maturity, the temple of the cinema began to rival in beauty, solidity, utility, and capacity the home of drama, the scene of light opera and musical comedy, the setting of the extravaganza, and the home of the melodrama."

The Stanley chain was the chief beneficiary of Hoffman & Henon's work, including the theaters in Baltimore (1927, razed) and Pittsburgh (1928). Their masterpiece was the monumental Philadelphia Mastbaum (1929, razed). The decoration was French Renaissance underscored by what might be called papal palatial. The massive neoclassical facade appeared far too staid to be a movie palace, but the initial appearance was deceptive; at night, color wheels were passed before floodlights set on top of the marquee, bathing the colossal Ionic colonnade in a variety of pastel shades.

Another architect working in the classical mode, at least in his early theaters, was C. Howard Crane. Perhaps the most prolific of the palace architects, Crane began his career in Detroit, with several theaters possessing some wonderful lobby spaces. The barrel vault over the small inner lobby of the Palms Theater (1921, now the Palms-State) is an intricate thing of beauty. The magnificent stained-glass

Hoffman & Henon's Mastbaum Theater (1929), *above*, offered Philadelphia moviegoers an elegant environment on a par with the city's prestigious nineteenth-century theaters. The grillwork cage, suspended above the stage apron, housed the sound system for the early talkies.

The terra-cotta decoration of the main facade of the Granada Theater (1926, shown under construction) was crowned by a tall dome when it was duplicated in another part of Chicago to front the Marbro Theater (1927). The monogramed canvas awnings beneath the Marbro marquee were necessitated by the cold Chicago winters.

ceiling above the grand foyer of Crane's Grand Circus (1922, now the Capitol) serves to balance the classical formalism of the exterior. For the lobby of the Allen Theater (1922) in Cleveland, Crane designed an elegant forty-five-foot-high rotunda patterned after that of the Villa Madonna in Rome. Crane's mastery of traditional styles and the classical design vocabulary was never in doubt, but his most notable theaters were built later, under the patronage of the studio chains.

Competing with Balaban and Katz in Chicago, the Marks Brothers exhibition firm hired architects Levy & Klein to design their theaters. Levy & Klein's earlier work in the city included the modest Diversey Theater (1924), built for the Orpheum vaudeville circuit, an organization known for cost cutting in their designs. Levy & Klein blended economy and opulence skillfully; the ornament molds used for the Granada (1926) were saved and re-used, with a few extra touches, for the chain's flagship, the Marbro (1927, razed). Both theaters were designed inside with a golden splendor rivaling the Vatican. The genius lay in their ability to achieve such spectacular effects with plaster.

Traditional picture palaces were every bit as popular on the West Coast, with several architects hard at work designing theaters. G. Albert Lans-

A web of Gothic vaultings decorates the outer lobby ceiling of the Golden Gate Theater (1921) in San Francisco.

burgh, the Beaux-Arts architect of the Salt Lake City Orpheum, set up shop in California. In San Francisco, Lansburgh overcame two difficult corner sites for the neighboring Golden Gate (1921) and Warfield (1922). The exquisitely pattern Gothic vaulting of the Golden Gate's outer lobby overpowers the theater's more conventional auditorium. These priorities were reversed in the Warfield, with an unexceptional lobby giving way to an auditorium topped by a boldly curving ceiling. Cove-lighted bull's-eye portals at the rear of the balcony ceiling are its final punctuation marks. Lansburgh's most completely developed theater is the Los Angeles Orpheum (1926), decorated throughout in rich French Renaissance style. The lobby is adorned in white marble; the auditorium is covered by a magnificent polychromed pattern of vaults and coves.

The architectural team of Weeks & Day also designed theaters throughout California, including some early links in the Fox chain. Most of their theaters had the atmosphere of a Gothic cathedral—expansive and severe. This ecclesiastical quality, climaxing in the San Diego Fox (1929), was enriched by a variety of late-medieval English design elements. The rows of pendants around the auditorium and the great central chandelier recall Hampton Court.

The theater opened on Dark Monday, ten days after the stock-market crash on Black Friday, but spirits were not yet depressed in San Diego. Celebrities arrived by train from Hollywood and paraded to the opening-night festivities. Inside, the celebration included an act high above the auditorium seats, with dancers from the Fanchon and Marco stage circuit kicking their heels in a circle around the central chandelier.

The San Diego Fox (1929), a Gothic-revival church masquerading as a movie palace. With the help of colorful lighting effects, the disguise is fully convincing.

Opening night speakers outside the San Diego Fox drew quite a crowd, despite recent news of the stock market crash back East.

One of the major attractions that night was the Fanchon and Marco stage act, shown in performance on a unique stage. To reach this perch the dancers had to climb down through the inside of the chandelier from the theater's attic.

The column-framed proscenium, canopy ceiling, and rounded side boxes of the Los Angeles Pantages (1921) were the trademark features of B. Marcus Priteca's "Pantages Greek" designs.

B. Marcus Priteca designed theaters for Alex Pantages's operation up and down the West Coast, beginning with the San Francisco Pantages in 1911 (razed). The similarities in the treatment of each theater's organ screens and proscenium arch were due to the preferences of Priteca's employer. The so-called Pantages Greek style was offset by the rich variety of ceiling coves. The broad murals painted around the rims of the coves centered on inset leaded-glass panels. For years this arrangement was standard in all Priteca theaters, from Los Angeles's Pantages Theater (1921) to the Mercy Theater

(1920, now the Capitol) more than a thousand miles to the north in Yakima, Washington.

Finally, in 1924, the San Diego Pantages (razed) was accorded a Spanish colonial treatment more appropriate to the city's history than classicism. Spanish carried the day again, with a vengeance, in the San Francisco Pantages (1926, now the Orpheum). Based on the fifteenth-century cathedral of León in Spain, the theater boasts decor that is almost oppressive in the extensiveness of its richly carved Moorish-Gothic ornamentation (labeled by some Inquisition Spanish).

When the public's taste changed at the peak of the golden age, even conservative firms built unusual theaters. Weeks & Day's most exotic theater was the Oakland Fox (1928), a Middle Eastern picture palace.

As with C. Howard Crane, Priteca's best work was done later, once he had freed himself from traditional decorative concepts.

The changes in style of the movie palaces were indirectly dictated by the public. Even in the early twenties there was a growing boredom with Old World styles. The country was changing fast—the postwar boom, the jazz age, flappers, prohibition—and its tastes changed just as fast. Americans wanted to live glamorous lives, and the movies began to reflect their desires. The time was ripe for the palace architects to throw away the old molds and join the spirit of the age.

# FANTASYLAND

Austrian-born architect John Eberson arrived in the Plains states at the turn of the century and set about making a name for himself. The named turned out to be "Opera House John," as Eberson became an architectural Johnny Appleseed for Sunbelt theatergoers. For twenty years Eberson built theaters in comfortably traditional

The Austin Majestic (1915), *above* and on *facing page*, is John Eberson's oldest theater. While a bit tame in comparison to his later designs, it has its own quiet charm.

styles, throwing in a few ceiling fans above the upper balcony to relieve summer hot spells. Two of the best of his traditional houses, the Austin Majestic (1915, now the Paramount) and the Dallas Majestic (1921), were designed for the Texas-based Hoblitzelle theater circuit. It was his design for the Hoblitzelle Majestic (1923, razed) in Houston that put Eberson in the national spotlight and shook the complacency of the traditionalists among the palace architects.

For the design of the Houston Majestic, Eberson replaced the stand-

ard ornate ceiling dome with a star-covered blue plaster sky. The twinkling electric constellations were occasionally obscured by clouds projected from a hidden Brenograph magic-lantern machine. Cumulus and nimbus clouds drifted lazily overhead in endless succession. The effect was achieved simply by passing a strip of negatives in front of a 1,500-watt light bulb,

The open-air illusion was enhanced by the stage-set walls encircling the auditorium, creating the feeling of being enclosed in an ancient Italian garden. Vines trailed over the walls

and, overhead, a few stuffed birds hung in mock flight. With this crowd-pleasing first act, John Eberson gave birth to the atmospheric theater.

The atmospheric theaters were extremely conducive to hosting the fantasy worlds that the film makers sought to create for theater patrons. As the name implies, an atmospheric contains within its make-believe walls the air of some distant and exotic outdoor arena.

The Houston Majestic was just a start. Atmospherics of every kind soon appeared; as composed by John Eberson: "We visualize and dream a magnif-

icent amphitheater, an Italian garden, a Persian court, a Spanish patio, or a mystic Egyptian templeyard, all canopied by a soft moonlit sky."

Eberson saw variety as "the primary demand of an amusement-loving public," and worked to fulfill that demand. Great pains were taken to ensure that the side walls in an Eberson theater never matched. He showed an inexhaustible capacity to blend decorative elements and rearrange statuary. Donatello's David or the Venus de Milo might have been present in a dozen Eberson theaters, but never in exactly

the same place or setting. Eberson went so far as to organize his own workshop, aptly titled Michelangelo Studios, in order to supply these plaster masterpieces for his theaters. Ben Hall was moved to call Eberson "an archaeologist, weatherman, and landscape gardener rolled into one."

For his design of the Chicago Capitol (1925), Eberson experimented with the atmospheric concept. He lowered the courtyard walls to bring the sky closer to the balcony patrons. For artistic inspiration, he credited "a few scattered examples of Greek and

The staggered trio of side boxes and the ceiling fans along the balcony front of the Houston Majestic (1923), *above*, were carryovers from John Eberson's earlier theaters.

Stacks of plaster ornament, *right*, courtesy of Michelangelo Studios, sit ready to be assembled as atmospheric side walls. The backdrop is the bare interior of the Loew's Akron (1929).

71

FANTASYLAND

The ornamental arrangement in the Chicago Capitol (1925), *left*, is much the same as that in the Houston Majestic. The Capitol's lower courtyard walls made the open-air illusion more convincing.

The Capitol's lobby, *below*, has a blue plaster sky to match the atmospheric auditorium.

Pompeiian architecture serving as standards." The end result bears a strong resemblance to the Italian garden interior of the Houston Majestic.

Eberson gave his Florida atmospherics a Spanish quality, in keeping with the state's early history. The lobby of the Olympia (1926, now the Gusman Center) in Miami features spiky chandeliers that appear to be of Inquisition vintage. The auditorium is disrupted slightly by a row of opera boxes along one sidewall, a throwback to Eberson's preatmospheric designs. The illusion is restored on the opposite wall, where the facade of a Castillian castle serves as an organ grill. A red-tiled parapet hangs over the proscenium opening.

The Tampa Theater (1926) was Eberson's favorite Mediterranean atmospheric, and one of his most intimate. Vines, flowers, and a strutting peacock decorate the walls of this Andalusian-Botanical wonderland. The plaster spectators scattered about the interior nearly outnumber the 1,500 seats. The opening-night program described many of the sculptures, which represent such varied characters as the goddess Diana and Queen Isabella's favorite explorer, Christopher Columbus.

Eberson's Spanish atmospherics were not confined to Florida. The State Theater (1927) in Kalamazoo, Michigan, has a rich Moorish exterior and hacienda organ grills. The asbestos fire curtain depicts a Spanish village, which appears to carry the side-wall architecture on through the proscenium arch. The chief attraction of Loew's United Artists (1928) in Louisville, Kentucky, is not its Spanish-styled auditorium but

Heraldic devices were incorporated into much of the surface decoration inside the Palace Theater (1928) in Marion, Ohio.

its long great hall. The plaster decoration of the barrel-vault lid is lined by medallion busts of famous historical figures, including one bust with Eberson's likeness.

Two of Eberson's best Spanish atmospherics are in Ohio. The auditorium of the Palace (1928) in Marion has the intimate scale of the Tampa Theater, without being as busy in its decoration. Even the housing for the projection booth above the rear of the balcony partakes of the Spanish atmosphere.

The overworked feeling of the Tampa Theater gives way to fantastic intricacy throughout the Loew's Akron (1929). The lobby has been replaced

by a great Moorish reception hall. The organ screens are now free standing, almost jutting into the auditorium. Gorgeous polychromatic ornaments cover the screens and zigzag across the proscenium arch. The quality of the Loew's Akron design was unmatched in all but the masterpieces Eberson built near the end of the golden age.

Unique among Eberson's early atmospherics is his Middle Eastern scheme for the Chicago Avalon (1927). It was inspired by a Persian incense burner that Eberson and Laska, his chief designer, spotted in a shop window on Royal Street in the French Quarter of New Orleans. Bulbous towers, somewhat incongruous on Chica-

The grand foyer of the Loew's Akron (1929), *above*, resembles a Moorish banquet hall.

Sharply detailed ornaments blend into powerful forms in the Loew's Akron auditorium.

*Facing page.* The summer of 1965 brought *Circus World* and *Beach Blanket Bingo* to the Avalon (1927), a Persian atmospheric theater on the south side of Chicago.

The Pilgrim's Fountain is tucked beneath pointed arches along the wall of the exotic Avalon.

go's south side, dominate the mosque-like exterior. The lobby originally contained a mirrored aquarium with more than 1,000 tropical fish.

Eberson's florid description of the Avalon auditorium neatly characterizes its excesses: "the richly grilled and torridly embellished palace on the left, the tall walls of a Persian rose garden on the right, the sacred pilgrim's fountain in the left side niche, the heavily barred and shuttered entrance to the sacred city courtyard on the right side of the main stage." The women's lounge.was designed as a harem parlor, the men's as a caliph's den. The ushers wore French Foreign Legion uniforms with plumed hats and white gloves.

Eberson's mix-and-match approach to theater architecture, combined with his passion for brightly colored lights (his most glaring weakness), left him open to charges of garishness and unwarranted eclecticism. Gaudy as they often are, Eberson's fanciful creations were still a welcome alternative to the formal elegance of the traditional palaces. The atmospherics were designed as places where, in Eberson's words, "our fancy is free to conjure endless tales of romance."

# CHANGES IN THE WEATHER

The brilliance of Eberson's stars and clouds was bound to inspire imitation. Claims have been made for the existence of an atmospheric theater prior to the Houston Majestic. When the Cort Theatre (razed), designed by J. E. O. Pridmore, opened in 1909, the Chicago *Evening American* reported "the whole effect is one of being outdoors with a warm Italian sky overhead." The atmospheric nature is undeniable, but the concept was not yet fully developed. The primary effects of the Cort were its blue, trellis-supported ceiling and trompe-l'oeil curtain. Tiers of opera boxes enclosed the auditorium in conventional fashion.

Later, Pridmore built an Eberson-style atmospheric, the Chicago Nortown (1931). Though far from any ocean, Pridmore chose to design the Nortown as a seafaring townscape. Prows guided by seahorses protrude from the organ screens. A lighthouse illuminates one wall and painted Span-

ish galleons circumnavigate the auditorium.

Architect Emile Weil adapted Eberson's idea to more formal designs in his theaters for the Saenger chain along the Gulf Coast. Finest among these is the New Orleans Saenger (1927), a Florentine garden under an Ebersonian plaster sky. The plaster walls are chiseled and painted to give the effect of heavy stonework. Perched atop these walls, a row of statues appear to view the proceedings in the manner of those above the piazza of St. Peter's in Rome.

Spanish atmospherics were popular in Texas, reflecting the state's blend of cultural histories. Texas's own W. Scott Dunne designed the Paramount (1927) in Abilene with a Spanish mission interior. Rounded towers along the side walls give the auditorium a hint of Byzantium.

Boasting that "royalty has its palaces, kings of finance their mansions, and Rockford has the Coronado," that

Illinois town opened its "wonder theater" in 1927. Predominantly Spanish in style, Frederic J. Klein's design for the Coronado is as eclectic as any theater by Eberson. A Moorish outer lobby leads into a foyer space covered in part by a two-story-high half dome. The decorative pattern of the semicircular ceiling consists of bright red, yellow, and green diamond shapes. The mirrors along the foyer wall are separated by a pair of nude figures for which the architect's wife is said to have modeled. The auditorium walls represent a castle with a combined Spanish and Byzantine flavor. The only thing Spanish about the organ grills, with their metallic golden dragons, is their intricacy, worthy of the Catalan master of sinuous art nouveau, Antonio Gaudí.

Before the golden age came to an end, a tremendous variety of atmospherics sprang up, some reflecting their locales, others transporting patrons to exotic lands. A white-steepled church

Although its atmospheric effects were relatively primitive, the Cort Theatre (1909), *right*, in Chicago can be considered a forerunner of the Houston Majestic, built fourteen years later.

*Facing page.* The Nortown Theater (1931), *top*, in Chicago was not quite ready to open at the time this photograph was taken. Drop cloths cover the seats and the organ shutters had not yet been draped, but the lighthouse was firmly set in its side-wall seascape.

The new Saenger Theater's bright marquee, *bottom*, was just part of the spectacle along Canal Street in New Orleans during Carnival Week in 1927.

Painted scenes infuse the Garden Theatre (1929) in Greenfield, Massachusetts, with a true New England atmosphere.

with a lighted clock tower presides over the quiet New England town painted on the sidewalls of the Garden Theatre (1929) in Greenfield, Massachusetts. Palm trees and a rainbow proscenium arch give the semiatmospheric Waikiki Theater (1936) in Honolulu an appropriately Hawaiian feeling.

Peter Hulsken, architect of the Holland Theater (1931) in Bellefontaine, Ohio, chose to design in the Dutch style simply because it was "Quaint, Picturesque, and different from any other atmospheric." The auditorium side walls were patterned after a seventeenth-century Dutch town, with step-gabled roofs and cross-bond brickwork. Final touches of authenticity include flower boxes filled with tulips and a pair of wooden windmills. Apparently following approximately the same logic as Hulsken, Elmer F. Behons designed the Pekin Theater in Pekin, Illinois, as an Oriental atmospheric. Multitiered pagodas bracketed

the stage, the hip rafters of each roof curled upward in traditional Oriental manner.

The most overpowering atmospheric of all is the Atlanta Fox (1929), known as the Fabulous Fox. Architects Mayre, Alger & Vinour were commissioned to build the Yaraab Temple, the new headquarters for Atlanta's Ancient Arabic Order of the Nobles of the Mystic Shrine. Architect P. Thorton Mayre, in 1928, characterized the Shriners' future home as a spectacle that would "out-Baghdad Baghdad." When the Shriners ran out of money, William Fox came to the rescue, with a lease for the building's auditorium as compensation. The Fox Building is a labyrinthine sprawl of rooms including shops, offices, Shriner halls, and an Egyptian ballroom. The Shriners scaled the theater's battlements only for their annual meeting; the rest of the year the Fox Theater was the domain of Atlanta's moviegoers. (The Shriners relinquished their

The imaginary Dutch town enclosing the auditorium of the Holland Theater (1931) in Bellefontaine, Ohio, appears to be perfectly inhabitable.

A shrine masks the organ chambers of the Pekin Theater, *right*, in Pekin, Illinois.

No atmospheric can match the great expanse of the Atlanta Fox (1929) auditorium, *bottom right*. Its seemingly impregnable walls keep the real world from disrupting the escapist pleasures offered within.

part ownership of the Fox in 1939.)

The patrons of the Fox are transported to the world of Ali Baba and *A Thousand and One Nights*, as depicted by the rhinestone-encrusted curtain strung across the broad proscenium opening. Wonderfully deceptive plasterwork is responsible for the sand-colored, rusticated fortifications rising along the side walls and, above the balcony, the red-and-yellow mock-canvas canopy that cuts across the desert sky. On the functional side, the plaster canopy disguises the air vents and conceals the special lights used to project the sunrise and sunset effects so popular at the Fox. In those few corners of the theater where the Arabian decor is absent, it is replaced by equally exotic features, from the Moorish box office to the colorful Egyptian women's lounge on the mezzanine level.

The Fox's exterior, with its onion-shaped domes, lancet arches, and minarets, is every bit as exotic as its auditorium. The set of fire exits along Ponce

de Leon Street are particularly unusual. In place of conventional, ugly metal fire escapes, the architects designed a massive masonry staircase. In keeping with the style of the exterior, the stairs are built (as Ben Hall coined it for posterity) from "ribbons of cream and buff brick." Since its opening on Christmas Day in 1929, the Fox has rested, like a fantastic mirage, to the north of downtown Atlanta, the mysterious "Mecca at Peachtree Street."

Unquestionably the most beautiful fire escape of any movie palace rises up the south wall of the Fox. The arched entry beneath the huge onion-shaped dome was originally the Shriners' access to their portion of the Fox Building.

# THE EXOTICS

John Eberson's first atmospherics were not the only surprising designs of the early twenties. In 1922, the unearthing of King Tutankhamen's tomb prompted a revival of ancient Egyptian architectural styles. In turn, this revival created a taste for the styles of other distant cultures from Central America to the Orient. A few maverick palace architects quickly moved to satisfy this cultural hunger with some of the most flamboyant theater architecture ever seen.

Hollywood's greatest showman, Sid Grauman, led the way in the Los Angeles area. Each of his theaters was unique, although imitations quickly followed. His first theater had been Grauman's Million Dollar (1918) in downtown Los Angeles. Covered with elaborate Spanish colonial ornamenta-

tion inside and out, the theater features a fabulously ornate terra-cotta arch over the main entrance on Broadway. At the manuals of the Million Dollar's Wurlitzer, organist Jesse Crawford started his career. From there he went on to make theater history with his masterful accompaniment of the silent films and his renditions of the popular songs of his day.

The architect of the Million Dollar, William Lee Woollett, also designed Grauman's Metropolitan (1923, became the Paramount in 1925, razed) in Los Angeles. Truly a one-of-a-kind theater, the Metropolitan had a blocky proscenium arch that verged on cubism. The lobby was simply bizarre, with a sphinx with the head of George Washington on a pedestal beside the lobby staircase. The quote near the base

of the sphinx read, "You cannot speak to us, O George Washington, but you can speak to God. Ask Him to make us good American citizens."

Once the movie business turned Hollywood into a boom town, Grauman decided to shift his operation away from downtown Los Angeles. Architects Meyer & Holler were commissioned in 1922 to build Grauman's Egyptian along Hollywood Boulevard. Entry to the theater requires passage through a forecourt lined with tall, rough-cut mock tombstones. During the show, an Egyptian guard marched back and forth across the roof parapet, rifle in hand. Inside the theater, a metallic vulture looms over the screen. The sunburst grillwork that extends from its wings masks the Egyptian organ screens.

This view of Grauman's Million Dollar in Los Angeles, taken shortly before the opening on February 1, 1918, shows the ruffled appearance of its Spanish colonial design.

The Egyptian style caught on quickly. Modified versions sprang up in unusual places, from Bala Cynwyd, Pennsylvania, to Coos Bay, Oregon. Frank Hunter's Zaring Theater (1925, razed) in Indianapolis had a broad-winged sounding board similar to the organ grill in Grauman's Egyptian. The Egyptian Theater (1927) in Boise, Idaho, has sphinxes perched on top of its roof. Inside, at either end of the stage, columns with lotus capitals frame a seated king. The columns are mod-eled after those in the temple at Karnak. Murals along the walls of the interior illustrate scenes from the Egyptian Book of the Dead. Architects Tourtel-lotte and Hummel added an atmos-pheric ceiling to complete their fantas-tic invention.

Hodgson & McClenahan's design for Peery's Egyptian Theatre (1924) in Ogden, Utah, covered the full range of Egyptian ornamentation. Lotus col-umns support the overhanging roof of the main facade, each column capped by sun disks, scarabs, and vulture wings. Six sculpted pharaohs serve as mullions. A pair of sculpted deities are seated on the roof with a matching pair sitting inside at the ends of the stage. When Peery's Egyptian opened, wisps of colored steam drifted from the bowls on the laps of these figures. The opening program credited the inspira-tion for the overall design to "the tem-ples built by Theban nobles about 1350 B.C." The slightly oppressive tomblike interior is relieved by its semi-

The interior of Grauman's Metropolitan (1923) in Los Angeles was an exotic jumble of Middle Eastern ornament and geometric patterning.

Few Egyptian-revival facades can compete with the front of Peery's Egyptian Theatre (1924) in Ogden, Utah.

The winged scarab sounding board is the only decoration not draped over in Grauman's Egyptian (1922) in Hollywood. Perhaps some future archaeologist will unearth the covered ornamental treasures of the auditorium.

atmospheric character, including constellations on the flat ceiling outlined by small electric lights. The program described the theater's special indirect lighting system, which was "used to simulate a night sky, golden sunsets, the silver light of dawn or moonlight." If all this did not wear out the patron, he could examine the hieroglyphics along the inner walls. Among the least authentic of the lines, incised in mock-ancient letters, was an unattributed quotation, "Harm Peery is a bum," apparently included just for fun.

Sid Grauman's last theater, one of the best known of all movie palaces, is Grauman's Chinese (1927) in Hollywood. Meyer & Holler's masterpiece opened with the premiere of Cecil B. DeMille's *King of Kings*, preceded by a special Sid Grauman prologue, "The Glories of the Scripture." The opening-night program described the theater's exterior: "A solid facade of masonry, 40 feet high, surmounted by four ornate obelisks, presents the effect of a huge gate or entrance to a great oriental garden, which opens to the view as a

gigantic elliptical forecourt . . . planted with full grown cocoa palms and rare tropical trees."

The forecourt has become more famous over the years as the site of some of the most unusual autographs of the Hollywood stars. The tradition of leaving hand- and footprints in the pavement began when Mary Pickford and Douglas Fairbanks accidentally walked in some wet cement before an opening.

The program also offered a grandiose description of the interior, in-

Crowds lined Hollywood Boulevard for blocks on the night of May 18, 1927 for the opening festivities of Grauman's Chinese Theater.

All 2,258 seats in the Chinese are on the main floor. The shelf balcony holds only the projection booth and Sid Grauman's private boxes.

cluding the chandelier: "A gigantic chandelier of bronze in the form of a colossal, round lantern, giving an effect of consummate grandeur by its extreme simplicity, its only ornament being rows of incandescent bulbs giving the effect of huge crystal strands." The ornate pagodas that originally bracketed the stage had to be removed once they began showing talkies at the Chinese. The sound apparently rattled the bronze and crystal, distracting the patrons.

While Grauman's Chinese may have been "Authentic in Every Detail," as chief designer Raymond Kennedy claimed, it is such a miscellaneous

assortment of popular Oriental furnishings that its style is more Chinese Chippendale than a representation of traditional Chinese architecture.

In contrast, the design carried out by R. C. Reamer in the Fifth Avenue Theater (1926) in Seattle is more faithful to its origins. The Fifth Avenue is the most exacting replication of all the movie palaces. The highly ornate auditorium is a near-perfect duplicate, at twice the original scale, of the throne room of the Imperial Palace in Peking's Forbidden City. The only detail Reamer changed was the color scheme of the carved "wooden" (plaster) beams. Forest green dominates a pattern of

The medallion-covered vault, *above*, receives special lighting above the great hall of the United Artists Theater (1928) in Louisville, Kentucky.

The Italian Renaissance found new expression along the walls of John Eberson's Loew's Paradise (1929), *left*, in the Bronx, New York.

A violet glow settles over the Majestic (1929), *left*, in San Antonio, Texas, John Eberson's final atmospheric creation.

These exotic creatures, *left*, gave a circus atmosphere to the Portland Oriental (1927). Primitive idols, *right*, frame a small tableau stage inside the Mayan Theater in Los Angeles.

A green-eyed god, *below*, half hidden by shadow, loomed above a royal procession on the Portland Oriental's asbestos curtain.

*Facing page*
The Moorish Gothic interior depicted by the rendering, *top left*, was never built.

Since a fire destroyed the proscenium arch of Albuquerque's KiMo Theater (1927), only this rendering, *top right*, remains as a record of the original decoration.

Lighted cow skulls cap the posts lining the KiMo's mezzanine promenade, *bottom*.

Facing page. Seattle's Fifth Avenue Theater (1926) in the midst of renovation for use as a legitimate theater.

One of a pair of golden warriors standing guard in the Detroit Fox lobby.

The smoky Byzantine auditorium of the Detroit Fox (1928).

The grand foyer staircase of the San Francisco Fox (1929), *right*, helped prepare patrons for the overpowering auditorium.

Simple painted plaster, *below*, takes magnificent shape in the Kansas City Midland's foyer (1927).

*Facing page.*
Thomas Lamb modified his design of the Oriental grand foyer, *top right*, in the Loew's State (1928) in Syracuse, New York, for use two years later in the Loew's 175th Street Theater (1930) in Manhattan, *top left*, the last of five Loew's "wonder theaters" built in the boroughs of New York.

Quotations from Reverend Ike fill in spaces along a foyer wall inside his United Church, *bottom*, the former Loew's 175th Street.

colors that Reamer "intentionally subdued for a Northwest flavor."

The fine draperies and furniture imported for the interior of the Fifth Avenue by Gump of San Francisco helped account for part of the theater's $1.5-million price tag. Assurances of authenticity were supplied by the team of artisans Reamer hired from among Seattle's Chinese population to do the plasterwork. One less authentic touch, borrowed from Sid Grauman, was the practice of outfitting the ushers in Oriental-style tunics and slacks.

The focus of the design of the Fifth Avenue is the great Golden Dragon, who radiates polychrome scales from

his position at the center of an eight-pointed star on the auditorium ceiling. Suspended from the dragon's mouth is the Pearl of Perfection (the central chandelier), which he is compelled to eternally seek but never grasp.

As with the Egyptian style, the influence of Grauman's Chinese was felt from coast to coast. The Oriental (1930, razed) in Mattapan Square, near Boston, borrowed from the architecture of China's Great Wall and Summer Palace. The overall scheme by Krokyn, Browne & Rosenstein featured organ grills modeled after a Tibetan shrine and the Temple of Five Pagodas, along with "a Foo dog gazing

The playful dragon on the asbestos curtain of Seattle's Fifth Avenue Theater (1926) balances the powerful character of the Chinese-Palatial auditorium.

The Loew's Ohio (1928) in Columbus features a brilliant red sounding board sprinkled with painted golden stars.

A Chinese-deco pagoda formed the main facade of the Oriental (1930), *above left*, in Mattapan Square, Massachusetts.

East Indian symbols decorate the auditorium of the Milwaukee Oriental (1928), *above right*.

*Facing page.* Lions growl silently by the lobby stairs of the Milwaukee Oriental while golden elephants support the ceiling.

down stonily from under the eaves" (*Motion Picture Herald*).

Matching ranks of bronze-colored Buddhas with glowing ruby-red eyes line the side walls of the auditorium of Dick & Bauer's Oriental (1928) in Milwaukee. The mock-tented ceiling, glowing in violet light, is supported by brackets formed by sculpted elephants and griffins. To complete the menagerie, eight black marble lions are regally posed in the lobby, alongside the staircase to the balcony.

The Portland Oriental (1927, razed) was built by G. W. Weatherly, a local dairyman, as an "East Indian playhouse." Architects Thomas & Mercier incorporated a few touches of the famous Cambodian temple at Angkor Wat into their design. Their playful composition included a pair of six-foot-tall golden Oriental dragons, seated on pedestals flanking the balcony staircase. Nestled safely in the dragons' laps were a pair of baby elephants, each with a royal headdress.

Inside the auditorium of the Portland Oriental, fourteen sacred elephants looked down between their tusks from positions high up on the side walls. Seven-headed serpents grew from the tops of the columns framing the stage. At the center of the proscenium arch was a huge primitive mask with glowing green eyes and a brilliant red mouth. Somehow even a collection of Egyptian mummies was added to the design, paired head-to-toe in a ring around the wildly ornate ceiling dome.

Balaban and Katz persuaded the Rapp brothers to design, somewhat reluctantly, a Far Eastern movie theater for Chicagoans. Rapp & Rapp, the purists among palace architects, felt that their pretentions to high culture and good taste would be compromised by gaudy Oriental exoticism. Nonetheless, B & K prevailed, and the architects loaded the walls to the limit with applied plasterwork elephants and chimeras. The advertising literature for the Chicago Oriental (1926) read: "Here is

A multitude of exotic animals presided over the lobbies and lounges of the Oriental (1927), *above*, in Portland, Oregon.

The auditorium of the Portland Oriental, *right*, is part circus, part pipe dream.

*Facing page.* This swirling view of the foyer of the Oriental Theater (1926) in Chicago shows why some critics consider the interior nightmarish.

romance agleam with modern theater magic, bringing to Chicago the jeweled splendor of the Far East against a backdrop of soft silk, subtle lights, and regal velvets."

The architects were not pleased. The office-block portion of the building, designed for Masonic groups in the Chicago area, was a technical marvel. With twenty-two floors of offices at the front of the building and Masonic halls ingeniously stacked at the rear, the Oriental Building was a structural success. But the auditorium remained an embarrassment to the firm. Rapp &

Rapp were reportedly so annoyed that, when the complimentary tickets to the theater's opening arrived, they tore them up.

The palace architects first turned to Central America for inspiration for the Aztec Theater (1926) in San Antonio, Texas. William Epstein, the theater's original owner, sent the architect, Robert B. Kelley, and his chief designer, R. A. Koenig, deep into Mexico to study the ruins of Aztec and Mayan cities. The Hall of Columns at Mitla served as the model for the foyer, with each column topped by a polychrome

Busy ornamentation covers the walls of the Chicago Oriental. All manner of plaster beasts compete for space above the organ screens.

Flowers filled the lobby of San Antonio's
Aztec Theater (1926) at its opening.

*Facing page.* The Aztec's auditorium decoration, *top*, centers around the blazing sun
symbol atop the proscenium arch.

The blocky exterior of the Denver Mayan
(1930), *bottom left*, is softened by polychrome ornaments and incised letters.

The original canopy marquee of the Los
Angeles Mayan (1927), *bottom right*, was a
perfect match for the decoration coating
the facade. The tall vertical marquee
looked more like an oil rig on the roof.

plaster mask representing the Aztec
goddess of the moon. The two-ton
chandelier suspended at the center of
the foyer ceiling is an exact replica of an
Aztec sacrificial calendar stone, complete with painted blood stains in the
drain grooves. The proscenium arch is
dominated by a plumed serpent, the
emblem of Quetzalcoatl, chief god of
the Aztecs. The scene on the fire curtain
depicts a properly dramatic moment in
Aztec history, the meeting of Cortez
and Montezuma.

Another lost culture whose architecture came to the attention of the
palace architects was the Mayan. The
Mayas had come to be viewed as the
Greeks of the New World. Their architecture was rediscovered by the modern world in the early part of the nineteenth century. Interest in Mayan styles
reached its peak at the 1893 World's
Fair. Lingering effects of these styles
surfaced again during the art deco period of the 1930s, but there was never a
full-scale revival of Mayan architecture
to match the periodic Egyptian revivals.

Nonetheless, moviegoers in
Denver and Los Angeles were treated

to reproductions of Mayan architecture, with decorative elements originally executed in cut stone now trans-
cribed into standard picture-palace
plasterwork. The facade of Morgan,
Walls & Clements's Mayan Theater
(1927) in downtown Los Angeles is
covered with serpent heads, celestial
symbols, and hieroglyphics. High
above the entry portal are carved seven
huge robed figures, each representing
Huitzilpochtli, the Mayan god of war.
The fantastic headdresses of these figures contain reflectors and floodlights.

The entrance lobby is an imitation
Hall of Inscriptions, coated with hieroglyphics, and the foyer is the Hall of
Feathered Serpents. The polychrome
plaster and metal of the auditorium's
calendar-stone chandelier is meant to
simulate antique copper encrusted with
verdigris jewels. The asbestos curtains
of the central stage and the two small
side stages look almost cartoonish to
modern eyes. The heavy outlines and
bright colors form a wild tropical vision
of Mayan kings and suppliants.

Industrial architect Albert Kahn's
famous Fisher Building in Detroit con-

THE PALACE ARCHITECTS

Before and after views of the Fisher Theater (1928) in Detroit. The 1928 view shows the orchestra in the pit and the Central American decor intact. The 1961 remodeling was executed by Rapp & Rapp.

A *Woman of Experience* was the opening show at the KiMo Theater (1927) in Albuquerque, New Mexico. To the left of the entry vestibule was the Kiva-Hi Cafe, decorated in Navajo style.

tains a theater originally decorated in Central American style. The Fisher Theater (1928) was designed by Mayger & Graven. The firm's other major palaces, including the Alabama (1927) in Birmingham and the Hollywood (1927, razed) in Detroit, were very tame in comparison with the colorful Fisher. The architects even planted banana trees in the foyer, in keeping with the Fisher's exotic nature. An uninspiring facelift was performed on the auditorium in 1961 by the firm of Rapp & Rapp. With the founding fathers long dead, the remodeling might be considered belated revenge for Rapp & Rapp's earlier run-in with the exotic rage.

Across the Cornbelt and the Southwest, the Boller Brothers perpetrated their own idiosyncratic styles of movie-palace design. The face of their Missouri Theater (1927) in St. Joseph resembles a Spanish cathedral. The interior could best be described as Greco-Babylonian, with side panels modeled after the ruins of Persepolis. The auditorium is semiatmospheric. A plaster circus tent with tassels hovers over the balcony to protect the audience from the imaginary elements. Robert Boller favored these "flame-proofed canopies to prevent reflection of tone and allow for the introduction of ventilation ducts from above, as well as indirect lighting of the house during intermission." (*Motion Picture News*)

The plaster tent in the auditorium of the Wild West-rococo Texas Theater (1926) in San Antonio appears to be tied to the walls of a Spanish patio straight out of Seville. Lighted by bright sunset hues, the star at the tent's center is meant to be the symbol of the Publix chain, but for local patrons it must have looked more like the badge of a Texas marshal.

Pablo Abeita, the former governor of Isleta Pueblo in New Mexico, was the man who named the Boller Brothers' theater in Albuquerque the KiMo (1927). The name, translated from the Indian dialect, means "king of its kind," which explains the KiMo's billing as "America's Foremost Indian Theater." The exterior was executed in a smooth, whitewashed stucco to imitate a Pueblo adobe. Brightly colored Navajo medallions run in bands beneath the second-story windows.

Inside the KiMo, longhorn skulls with flashing electric eyes crown the lobby pillars and line the auditorium walls. Among the ornamental details lost to a fire in the 1970s were the plaster Navajo rugs that hung alongside the stage and the chandeliers designed to represent Indian farewell canoes.

The Plaza Theater (1929) in Kansas City, Missouri, was designed as the anchor theater of America's first major shopping center, J. C. Nichols's Country Club Plaza. The Plaza Theater's Spanish colonial exterior is in keeping with the predominant stylistic theme of the shopping center, but the auditorium continues the exotic trend begun in earlier Boller Brothers theaters.

A lavish bell tower crowns the exterior of the Boller Brothers' Plaza Theater (1929) on the outskirts of Kansas City, Missouri.

Robert Boller is quoted in a 1929 *Motion Picture News* article as favoring conventional styles for theater design, while "unusual and faddish styles will come and go." The statement seems almost absurd in light of the Boller Brothers' previous eccentric design history.

Understandably, exoticism was too much for the traditional palace architects. Paul J. Henon of Hoffman & Henon lodged the following complaint in 1928: "If the theatergoer is to be shocked at the outset by some grotesque ornamentation, he will never be in the proper frame of mind to enjoy what is presented to him in the way of entertainment. He will unconsciously develop an aversion to that particular playhouse. It will never know him more as patron."

The daily counts proved Henon wrong.

# MASTERS IN MATURITY

During those years when the Boller Brothers and Meyer & Holler catered to the wildest fantasies of movie patrons, the old guard was not out of work. The major architects adapted the new mix of styles to their own ends, building some of the most romantic structures ever seen, not all of them movie palaces. Lamb, Eberson, and Rapp & Rapp each had their share of nontheatrical commissions, but there are unmistakable signs in these buildings that the heart of their architectural practices lay with the gaudy movie houses.

The onion-domed exterior of the Corn Palace exhibition hall in Mitchell, South Dakota is the work of none other than Rapp & Rapp. After the original 1892 building was demolished, they designed the present hall in 1921, the same year the Tivoli and the Chicago Theater were opened. (Showing the strength of their ties to B & K, Rapp & Rapp designed the Balaban family mausoleum in Waldheim Cemetery near Chicago.)

Ballrooms were big business in the twenties, and Chicago had two of the best, courtesy of the palace architects.

Rapp & Rapp's elegant Trianon Ballroom (1921, razed) showed their French palatial style in all its richness. A second-level tier of boxes ringed the dance floor in a manner that recalled their design of the Ringling Memorial in Baraboo. Eberson's atmospheric style worked beautifully in the Aragon Ballroom (1926), perhaps even better than in his theaters. The dance floor of this luxuriously romantic "dance castle" is encircled by a cluster of whitewashed Mediterranean villas, with balconies raised on a grand arcade. The elliptical wood floor has a listed capac-

ity of 6,000, but an opening night crowd of 8,000 was safely carried on the ingenious spring-suspension system built beneath the floor. The architects of record were local partners, Huzach & Hill, but Eberson's touch in this Spanish fairyland is unmistakable.

Thomas Lamb permitted himself an Egyptian fling in his design of New York's Pythian Temple (1927). A playful jumble of Egyptian elements is strewn across the front facade of a tall, office-block frame. The temple's auditorium and lodge rooms were not designed with quite the same flair, but the

lobby (altered in the sixties) was a real surprise. The polished black marble columns and the golden stylized sun disks and vulture symbols mixed Egyptian elements in an art deco fashion, although art deco was still years away for most palace architects.

Lamb's fame, nationally and internationally, ultimately took him to Moscow, although not to design a movie palace. He was invited to submit an entry to the 1932 design competition for a Palace of the Soviets. Lamb's design appears, from his drawings, to be a geometric arrangement of huge blocks

and cylindrical forms, alternating in a line. His entry was not chosen, but it did earn him an honorable mention.

Despite these outside projects, the major palace architects had not lost interest in theater building. Lamb, Eberson, and the Rapp brothers each designed a staggering number of theaters in the late twenties. Hoover and the Depression were just around the corner and vaudeville was dying, but the movie industry was booming. In 1928 alone, these three firms built more than twenty major theaters, including some of their best. In order to get those commissions, the architects, especially Lamb and the Rapp brothers, were forced to abandon much of their conventional decorative treatments and adapt themselves to the changing tastes of the moviegoing public. The traditional picture palaces gave way to more exotic theaters, but not before the grandest of the old-style movie houses was built; New York's Roxy Theatre (1927, razed).

With the Roxy, as Ben Hall put it, "the gaudy, enchanting, phony, preposterous, and lovely Golden Age of the Movie Palace reached its Klieg-lit pinnacle." Architect W. W. Ahlschlager designed the Roxy as more than just a movie theater. He incorporated into its design a complete hospital, the largest musical library of any theater, and a modern refrigeration and ventilation system. The air in the vents was

Rapp & Rapp's favorite French-palatial style was used to good effect in Chicago's Trianon Ballroom (1921). La Salle de Spectacle at Versailles served as the architects' inspiration.

washed as it passed through special chambers outfitted with nozzles spraying atomized water. The advertising literature for the Roxy boasted of a lighting plant "sufficient to power a city of a quarter million," a number far in excess of even the Roxy's capacity crowd of 5,920.

The auditorium space was cavernous. Ahlschlager explained how he tried to offset the feeling of sprawl by varying the size of the architectural or-

John Eberson's flamboyant tendencies are fully realized in another Chicago night-spot, the Aragon Ballroom (1926). The Spanish arcade ringing the dance floor ranks among Eberson's most beautiful creations.

nament in different areas: "Each thousand is seated in its own environment, with the surrounding architecture brought down to the scale of that particular thousand. The proscenium enframement was so designed as to tie all these divisions into one architecutral phantasy." Ahlschlager's other design illusion was the color scheme, chosen to draw the walls together rather than to allow them to recede. Accordingly, supervising decorator Harold W.

Rambusch designed the Roxy as "the inside of a great bronze bowl."

Beyond the contributions of the architect and the decorator, the theater's overall design scheme was the product of Roxy Rothafel, the acknowledged high priest of New York's movie palaces. The religious trappings of the "Cathedral of the Motion Picture" included a set of tower chimes, a grand dome encircled by a spotlight gallery, and pulpits alongside the stage, reached by curving golden stairways suspended below them.

Before reaching the cathedral interior, the patron passed through the awe-inspiring rotunda, which rose five-stories. Twelve columns of green marble, topped by a circular chariot-race frieze, supported the rotunda's high dome. Spread across the floor was "the largest oval rug ever woven to order," measuring fifty-eight feet by forty feet and weighing more than two tons.

The rotunda was a favorite of Ahlschlager's. He had used it before in the Chicago Belmont (1926), and employed it later in the lobby of the somewhat bizarre Beacon (1929) on Manhattan's Upper West Side. The Beacon has an overall conquistador motif. The most notable feature of the interior is the broad proscenium awning supported on the lances of two tall Indian warriors, who stand on pedestals flanking the stage.

*Facing page.* The view above this ocean of seats from inside the spotlight gallery (just visible at the top) must have been amazing. Roxy's private box was perched above the rear of the balcony inside New York's Roxy Theatre (1927).

The Roxy rotunda, *above*, was as regal as any reception room ever built.

The rotunda inside Chicago's Belmont Theater (1926), *top right*, is smaller than the Roxy rotunda but no less elegant.

Conquistadors rule the side walls of New York's Beacon Theater (1929), *bottom right*, but the vanquished Indians flank the stage opening.

*Facing page.* The origins of the decorative elements C. Howard Crane used for the United Artists (1927) in Los Angeles are in nineteenth-century English architecture, particularly the Houses of Parliament. Crane's exotic arrangement of the Gothic elements was without precedent.

One member of the old guard, C. Howard Crane, built his best theaters in the late twenties, but they were quite different from his earlier classical output. Crane first hit his stride in the designs for United Artists, then run by Mary Pickford and Douglas Fairbanks. He built the first United Artists Theater (1927) in Los Angeles for Pickford. What appear to be plaster stalactites are clustered above the organ screens and the proscenium opening. The decorativeness recalls the intricately carved, carpenter-Gothic designs of the mid-nineteenth-century arts and crafts movement. Painted along the side walls are murals showing the United Artists stars in their most famous roles, including Pickford herself as "America's Sweetheart."

The following year, Crane used similar decorative effects to revamp the Apollo Theatre (1921, by Chicagoans

Holabird & Roche) as the new Chicago United Artists. For Detroit's United Artists (1928), Crane used a few Indian maidens to distinguish this theater and its auditorium from the cave-Gothic interior of the Los Angeles movie house.

Crane is best known for the twin 5,000-plus seat movie palaces he designed for the Fox chain. The Detroit Fox (1928) differed from the St. Louis Fox (1929) only by the treatment of its facade and a handful of seats (the Detroit Fox has six more). The lobbies of the two theaters are filled with molded plaster ornament, made to resemble burnished metal. Some of the more prominent details are the *e pluribus unum* eagles decorating the bases of the blood-red support columns, and the vultures joined to form the capitals of the columns. Golden Turkish warriors with scimitars guard the lobby staircases in both theaters. On the lobby landings are Persian throne chairs with camel armrests. Ben Hall labeled the auditoriums Siamese-Byzantine; tusked golden elephants gaze down from atop the proscenium arches. Both theaters' ceilings feature an earth-colored circus tent from the center of which hangs a massive glowing ball of lights on a col-ored glass frame sixteen feet in diameter. (Relamping—the changing of the bulbs—is accomplished by scaling ladders contained within the twin chandeliers.)

Thomas Lamb made the transition to exotic theater design in steps. The Albee Theater (1925, razed) in Brooklyn, New York, showed Lamb still in his Adamesque period. Both the Fountain Square facade and the auditorium of the Cincinnati Albee (1927, razed) reflected a shift in Lamb's classical treatment to the Palladian classicism of sixteenth-century Italy. The towering grand foyer showed hints of the mix-

Pairs of monkeys and serpent arches stand out from the temple fronts lining the auditorium walls of the Detroit Fox, *right*.

*Facing page.* All the glories of the East, far and near, appear to be packed within the walls of the lobby of the Detroit Fox (1928).

The arches at either end of the mezzanine colonnade inside Cincinnati's Albee Theater (1927) echoed the monumental Palladian arch cut into the main facade.

The formal lines of the Albee's foyer walls gave way to the fluid curves of the rococo ceiling.

ture of baroque and French rococo elements that Lamb used to create his most palatial theaters.

The first theater in Lamb's barococo style was the Loew's Midland (1927) in Kansas City, Missouri. The theater was thoroughly filled with royal splendors. The plush lobby contains a rich variety of antique finery, furnishings, and art objects among the plaster cherubs and Corinthian columns. The

Oriental room of W. K. Vanderbilt's demolished Manhattan townhouse was brought to Kansas City and reassembled in the Midland as a women's lounge. Inside the auditorium, the organ screens are powerfully massed baroque compositions shaded a dark brown. A crown, the symbol of the city, rests at the peak of the proscenium.

The Midland was reportedly Marcus Loew's favorite theater, and the

price was steep. The building plus furnishings cost well over $3 million. Six-and-a-half million square inches of gold and silver leaf were used on the walls and ceilings. Lamb boasted of the Midland, "It has set a standard so high that it will be found difficult to maintain."

Indeed, only one other theater stands out from Lamb's short-lived barococo period, but what a theater! The San Francisco Fox (1929, razed) was

The proscenium arch of the regal Loew's Midland (1927) in Kansas City, Missouri, was designed to accommodate this unusual arrangement of the grand drape beneath a huge crown.

The rich barococo organ screens of the San Francisco Fox (1929) climbed to dizzying heights.

Lamb's opening-night spectacular in comparison with the full dress rehearsal of the Kansas City Midland. The organ screens in the Fox, while strongly reminiscent of those in the Midland, towered far higher above the orchestra floor. The grouped columns around each screen supported a wonderful mass of intricate ornamentation arranged in a composition equaling those of the baroque masters centuries be-

San Francisco's Market Street was filled to capacity one summer evening in 1929 for the formal opening of Thomas Lamb's only West Coast palace.

fore. The patterning of the organ screens was repeated by the terra-cotta cladding around the magnificent arch that rose above the Fox's Market Street entry doors.

The lobbies and promenades of the Fox resembled a lavish art museum. A grand foyer staircase worthy of the Paris Opéra carried patrons into the largest and grandest movie palace ever built on the West Coast.

The second branch of Lamb's new palace designs came to fruition with the Loew's Ohio (1928) in Columbus. The glorious interior decoration was referred to by his office as "a faithfully carried-out Mexican baroque." Lamb felt that this design blended "the sumptuousness of Spain, and the intricacy and construction of our modern art." By modern art he meant art deco, which was hinted at in the design of the auditorium sounding board: ". . . a mosaic of gold, silver, and red, of such complexity that it defies the mind to discover the pattern on which it is built. Its effectiveness lies in its texture of metal stars spattered and superimposed upon a ground of red."

The Rambusch Decorators, working with Lamb, were the creators of this design. Although they were well aware of art deco, they located the inspiration for the star pattern in "an Islamic interlace pierced sun screen." The geometric forms included along the proscenium arch and the side bays evolve from Moorish baroque.

The focal point of the auditorium ceiling is a large eight-pointed star of stained glass, illuminated from above. From the center of the star hangs an elegant chandelier. Legend has it that the first sight of the chandelier moved Lamb to say, "I don't believe it! This thing has everything on it but flying horses!" The oversight was then quickly rectified by the chandelier's designer, as a flock of miniature crystal

As if awakening from a bad dream to a glorious dawn, the flattened-wallpaper quality of the Loew's Canal (1927) in New York gave way to the supreme richness of the Loew's Ohio (1928) in Columbus.

The same devilish faces as those in the Loew's Ohio peer out from the organ screens of the Stanley Theater (1928) in Utica, New York.

Pegasuses were added around the bottom of the fixture. (The veracity of this story is seriously jeopardized by the presence of a duplicate of the chandelier, complete with flying horses, in the rotunda of the Belmont Theater in Chicago, built two years before the Ohio.)

The designer responsible for most of the furnishings in the Ohio was Anne Dornan, one of the first women to graduate from Columbia's School of Architecture. Her budget for decorating the Ohio was said to have been

nearly $1 million. Included in this sum was a trip around the world, from which Dornan returned with such artifacts as those that decorated the safari-style Africa Corner (the room no longer exists).

Certain grandiose design elements, including portions of the Ohio's organ screens and proscenium arch, reappeared in the Stanley Theater in Utica, New York and in the Keith's theaters in Flushing, New York, and Huntington, West Virginia (all built in 1928).

Lamb, like Crane with his Fox designs, had learned the economy of duplication. Lamb cut even more corners for the two Keith's theaters by eliminating the ornate ceiling he had used in the Loew's Ohio. The Keith's were among a handful of atmospherics he designed. Lamb considered the atmospheric brand of theater no more than a novelty item—"my personal opinion is that this type of work will not be lasting"—but he gave his clients what they asked for.

The baroque interior of the Keith's (1928) in Huntington, West Virginia, is a low-budget version of the Loew's Ohio.

None of Thomas Lamb's atmospherics, including the Triboro (1931) in Astoria, New York, could match the romantic inspiration of Eberson's theaters.

THE PALACE ARCHITECTS

Lamb's last great palaces are "permeated with a touch of the Orient—brightly colorful, emotional, and almost seductive" *(Motion Picture News)*. The burnished bronze look of the Syracuse Loew's State (1928) was characterized by Lamb as "European Byzantine Romanesque, the Orient as it came to us through the merchants of Venice." Lamb was proudest of all of the grand foyer, "a temple of gold set with colored jewels."

The chandelier that originally hung in the foyer was another item the Loew's organization had salvaged from Vanderbilt's townhouse. The great central pendulum of stained glass was surrounded by smaller sconces with the same exotic bulbous form. Misguided concern during World War II that an enemy bombing of Syracuse might cause the chandelier to fall led to the fixture's removal. (It has since been sold in pieces, with orphaned sconces now on the living room walls of some American celebrities.)

Lamb hired Scottish craftsmen to do the theater's plasterwork ornament. The workers copied much of the design directly from scholarly works on Far Eastern architecure and art. The origin of the massive scrolled columns of the foyer can be directly traced to ancient columns from Hindu temples.

Loew's 175th Street Theater (1930) in New York contains a virtual

An extraordinary glass chandelier from the demolished Vanderbilt mansion found its way into the foyer of the Loew's State (1928) in Syracuse, New York.

Thomas Lamb built this promenade in triplicate—one for each of his Oriental palaces. A comparison of this version, in the Loew's 175th Street (1930) in New York, with the plush marble-lined mezzanine promenade of the Poli Palace in Worcester, Massachusetts (1926), shows how versatile Lamb could be.

duplicate of the interior of the Syracuse theater, including the auditorium, "a vast hood of gold surrounded by an elaborate network of lacing and interlacing ornament." The one major difference is that the solid ornamental side walls of the Loew's State have been replaced by a free-standing grill, illuminated from behind by concealed multicolored lights.

The exterior of the Loew's 175th Street has a rich geometric blockiness that shows both Mayan and art deco influences. Lamb had tested this styling the year before on the exterior of the Loew's Pitkin in Brooklyn. The Pitkin is a Lamb hybrid; it has a Mexican baroque atmospheric enclosed within the

same ornamental blocks as those forming the shell of Loew's 175th Street.

The last of Lamb's Far Eastern gems was Loew's 72nd Street Theater (1932, razed) in New York. The decorative treatment in the foyer was essentially the same as it has been in both the Loew's State and at Loew's 175th Street. The auditorium, however, was something new. Here Lamb created an Indochinese atmospheric inspired by the great tower of the pagoda of Wat Ching in Cambodia. Grillwork temples were set in the side bays. Above the proscenium arch a huge, bulbous lantern smoldered. (Moviegoers in the sixties might conceivably have mistaken the lantern for a flying saucer.)

Primitive Mayan touches decorate the monumental blocks of the Loew's 175th Street's exterior.

Lamb's 175th Street Theater had been the last of the famed "Loew's wonder theaters" to open in the New York area. The other four were built in 1929, with the commissions split evenly between John Eberson and the Rapp brothers. All major Loew's commissions had gone to Lamb in the past, but the inspiration for the wonder theaters did not lie with Loew's. The original plan, to build five huge picture palaces in the outlying boroughs of New York, was a Paramount project. (William Fox realized a similar plan on a nationwide scale in the late twenties, with major Fox theaters in Detroit, St. Louis, Atlanta, Brooklyn, and San Francisco.)

A dramatic air of foreboding filled the temples of Thomas Lamb's last big movie palace, the Loew's 72nd Street (1932) in New York.

The crown shape Thomas Lamb had used inside the Kansas City Midland, *right*, became a pedestal for the glowing lantern above the stage of the Loew's 72nd Street.

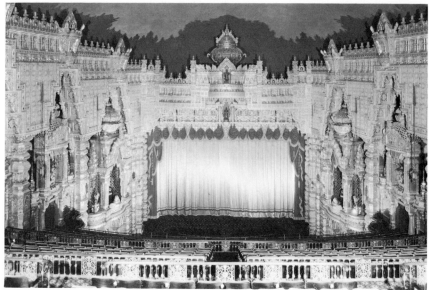

*Facing page.* Among all of John Eberson's atmospherics, only the Loew's Akron can match the balance and grace of the Spanish colonial interior of Loew's Valencia (1929), *top*, in Queens, New York.

Artificial clouds (the photograph is a double exposure) and a trompe-l'oeil curtain heighten the atmospheric illusion of the stage arch inside the Loew's Paradise (1929), *bottom*, in the Bronx, New York. John Eberson's side-wall plasterwork is equally surrealistic.

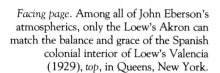

When financial troubles kept Paramount from following through with the wonder theaters, Loew's bought the project, complete with the four sets of blueprints done for Paramount by Eberson and Rapp & Rapp. Thomas Lamb was hired to add the final theater.

Eberson's two wonder theaters live up to this special classification. The Spanish cathedral atmosphere of the Loew's Valencia (1929) has a richness that is surprisingly restrained. Eberson had learned to control his more garish impulses. He arranged the interior of the Valencia with a graceful rhythm that had been lacking in his earlier Spanish atmospherics. Exotic touches are still in evidence, though; particularly in the lobbies, where lion-head capitals crown every column and post along the plasterwork arcades.

Maidens and musclemen hold up the vine-draped roof of Lorenzo de Medici's private box at the Loew's Paradise. Pigeons populate the side wall ledge.

Eberson's impulses were at their most unrestrained when he designed the Loew's Paradise (1929) in the Bronx, New York, but no one could object. The composition of the auditorium is as cluttered as the design he used three years earlier for the Tampa Theater, but on a much grander scale. Busts of notables from William Shakespeare to Benjamin Franklin are set in individual niches. Pigeons flock around the statuary as if in Venice, and vines trail down every wall. The interior recalls the Italian Renaissance in its fullest flower, with beautiful statuary outlining the proscenium arch and clustered

at the organ screens. The classical ornaments heaped around the organ screens are the atmospheric equivalent of Thomas Lamb's grandiose design elements piled high along the sidewalls of the San Francisco Fox. The greatest mystery in the Paradise is how anyone can watch the movie with everything else to see.

The Paradise exterior fronts on the Grand Concourse, the Bronx's main thoroughfare. The facade was limited by local ordinances to maintain a flat surface, but even here the ornament draws the eye. Above a clock in the wall above the marquee, St. George slays the

dragon every hour on the hour.

The Bronx Paradise was the second of Eberson's heavenly atmospherics. The Chicago Paradise (1928, razed), a more ethereal version, had been built the preceding year. The interior of the Chicago Paradise was breathtaking. The outer lobby rose skyward, its blue plaster ceiling dotted with ghostly murals showing figures representing the signs of the zodiac. The auditorium must have appeared to be heaven on earth. Eberson allowed the sky to drop all the way to the "horizon" behind free-standing walls, for the fullest atmospheric effect.

In place of the usual electric stars, the constellations were painted and illustrated on the atmospheric ceiling of the outer lobby in the Chicago Paradise (1928). Some fine-feathered specimens strut above the bronze entry doors.

Above the delicately worked proscenium arch, a golden chariot mural described a dawn of near-apocalyptic proportions. Three full-size white plaster steeds, perched above the proscenium, appeared ready to gallop over the arch into the auditorium. It was not without some justification that the owners, Balaban and Katz, billed the Chicago Paradise as "The World's Most Beautiful Theater."

The exterior of this Paradise certainly lived up to its billing. If Eberson's aim had been to duplicate the finest elements of Second Empire architecture, he could not have done any better.

The beautiful formal rhythm of the main facade was capped by a tall mansard roof with a slight convex curve. The high tower built above the outer lobby stood out from the long main facade, matching the rise of the vertical marquee from the ornate canopy marquee. The exterior of the Chicago Paradise ranked with the finest theater facades ever built.

For his last palace, Eberson returned to Texas, the site of his first atmospheric, and built the towering false-front walls of the San Antonio Majestic (1929). His old boss, impresario Karl Hoblitzelle, claimed the Majes-

tic "will be made as great an influence for good as the church." It barely had a chance. The theater opened at the beginning of Prosperity Month in San Antonio, when business was booming. Four months later, Black Friday ushered in the Depression.

The design of the Majestic's auditorium shows Eberson's preferred asymmetry. The left wall was modeled after a Spanish colonial *palacio*, the right wall drawn from a Moorish castle. Among the usual flock of stuffed birds, Eberson included a few Texas turkeys. As a final bow to San Antonio's proud heritage, Alamo bells hang against a

THE PALACE ARCHITECTS

The auditorium of the Chicago Paradise
was an unearthly mixture of tranquil
beauty and explosive power.

The fancy marquee of the Loew's Paradise
(1928) in Chicago, Illinois.

The facades of John Eberson's theaters were often as spectacular as the atmospheric interiors. The polychrome terracotta and dark brick exterior of the Loew's Richmond (1928), Virginia, outshines anything inside the theater.

The Alamo bells atop the proscenium of the San Antonio Majestic (1929) recall the city's origins. The use of staggered side boxes dates back to John Eberson's earlier Texas theaters. The second balcony (for Blacks) is an ugly reminder of the racial discrimination that endured well into the twentieth century.

A broad marble staircase and crystal chandeliers were among the extravagant appointments in the New York Paramount (1926).

bright purple sky. Remember the Alamo? Eberson practically re-created it!

Even before they designed their pair of Wonder Theaters, the Rapp brothers were not unknown in New York. Most people, including C. W. Rapp himself, consider the Chicago Theater the firm's best work, but the Paramount (1926, razed) on Times Square was undoubtedly their richest theater. (The theater was destroyed in 1964, though the building still stands.) A triumphal arch on the square marked the entry. The low ceiling of the Hall of Nations opened into the imposing Grand Hall. Over $500,000 worth of marble was used to build the columns that ringed this space. A quarry in Italy that had been closed for forty years was reopened to fill the order for the stone.

The French Renaissance auditorium contained a gallery promenade built into the ceiling dome. The promenade was meant for use by patrons awaiting the next show. Eventually the theater management was forced to close the area because of noise drifting down into the auditorium.

The exterior of the Paramount has always been a prominent sight on Times Square. Broadway's first great clock tower caps a series of setbacks. A flashing sphere, a globe intended to symbolize world conquest by the motion picture, is perched on top of the

The Paramount's constricted Times Square site made for a tall, narrow auditorium, unusual in a Rapp & Rapp theater.

building, 450 feet above street level. The globe is fourteen feet in diameter, with ninety squares of glass sheeted with copper. It was designed to indicate the hour by a flash of color, red for odd hours and white for even.

Rapp & Rapp's wonder theaters possess a richness of ornament nearly equal to the Times Square Paramount. The Loew's Kings Theater (1929), although named for its location in Kings County (Brooklyn), was nonetheless designed for royalty. The auditorium has a majestic expanse, low and flat, with only a short shelf balcony. The equally impressive grand lobby was decorated in French baroque, with murals and sculpted plasterwork along the walls and ceiling.

The other Rapp wonder theater is the Loew's Jersey (1929) in Jersey City, New Jersey. Its main facade, overlooking Journal Square, has a powerful severity of expression. There is a strong vertical emphasis to the design, and yet another St. George clock tower, matching the one on Eberson's wonder theater in the Bronx.

At the end of the thirties, Rapp & Rapp adopted a few atmospheric measures. They justified these on the grounds that "theatergoers in the big cities need foliage, water displays, etc., to counteract urban congestion." The Toledo Paramount (1928, razed) and the Gateway (1930) in Chicago were

Every feature of the facade of the Loew's Jersey (1929), *above*, in Jersey City, New Jersey, appears to be straining skyward.

The Jersey's barococo interior has much in common with Thomas Lamb's San Francisco Fox, *right*, built the same year three thousand miles away.

*Facing page.* The Toledo Paramount (1928) was a rarity; a Rapp & Rapp atmospheric, more elegant if less fanciful than John Eberson's theaters.

Rapp & Rapp's only fully atmospheric houses, but an Ebersonian influence is also apparent in the designs of the firm's last traditional palaces, the Brooklyn Paramount (1928) and the Southtown (1931) in Chicago.

The Brooklyn Paramount was seen by its chief designer, Arthur Frederick Adams, as "a composite palace," the perfect blend of atmospheric and conventional theaters. Trees and potted plants against the sky-blue backdrops of the ornate side bays give a semi-atmospheric feeling to the auditorium. Rapp & Rapp's version of the blue plaster sky common to Eberson's

Rapp & Rapp appropriated the sun sign, symbol of Louis XIV, for their own. The Brooklyn Paramount (1928) possesses a magnificent cove dawn.

theaters is a back-lighted latticework trellis hovering above the balcony. A masterly touch, attributable solely to Rapp & Rapp, is the royal sunburst over the proscenium arch illuminated by hidden cove lights.

Atmospheric side bays and free-standing organ screens give the side walls of the Southtown Theater the character of an enclosed Italian garden. The lobby bays and niches celebrate Chicago history with dioramas showing such familiar local sights as the

stockyard, and such memorable moments as the 1893 World's Columbian Exposition and the Great Fire of 1871.

The Southtown was the last palatial design built by Rapp & Rapp, but not their last theater. The waning years of the twenties had seen increasing interest in art deco. Traces of the new style had begun to appear on the drawing boards of Rapp & Rapp as early as 1928. When art deco came to full flower in the early thirties, Rapp & Rapp were well prepared.

Chicago's Southtown Theater (1931) has the same composite arrangement as the Brooklyn Paramount, but at a lower price. Stenciled ornaments replaced plaster cast.

Rapp & Rapp turned John Eberson's conception upside-down in the Brooklyn Paramount, doming atmospheric side walls with an ornamental ceiling.

# YEARS OF TRANSITION

Although architects showing in the Paris Exposition of Decorative Art gave birth to the style in 1925, it took time for art deco to be absorbed by the palace architects. They did utilize the streamlined geometric forms of art deco in some late 1920s' theaters, but the mixed qualities of jungle primitivism and machine-inspired design that originated at the Paris exposition were not apparent in American movie theaters until 1930. The intervening years provide a number of noteworthy transitional theaters, the majority of them in the Los Angeles area.

Dwight Gibbs's Carthay Circle (1926, razed) in Los Angeles showed the earliest traces of art deco in its streamlined exterior. The theater's tall mission-style tower was like a beacon in the night sky, drawing customers from all around the city to the Carthay Circle. The theater was best known as the site of some of the first major movie premieres. Warner Brothers went as far as to stage a big premiere in front of the Carthay Circle as a backdrop for the pivotal scene in *Boy Meets Girl* (1938).

The mission tower and whitewashed stucco exterior of the Carthay Circle became trademark features of the Fox–West Coast theater operation. The Fox (1929) in Riverside has a blocky mission exterior, designed by Balch and Stanbury, but no great tower. S. Charles Lee built the Fox (1932, razed) in Florence, California, as a Spanish Colonial villa. The entry to the theater was under a low arch onto a tile patio. A broad staircase curved around the patio, carrying patrons to the lobby doors on the landing above.

The high point of mission revival

was reached by Plunkett & Edwards in the Fox-Arlington (1931) in Santa Barbara. The theater's tall white tower, copied from the Alcazar of Segovia, Spain, marks its location. As Santa Barbara's largest building, the Fox-Arlington could easily be mistaken from a distance to be a historical mission. Even the fire escapes (since demolished) were designed to look like white stucco steps. The neon ruffles of the canopy marquee and the revolving Fox sign around the pinnacle of the tower, however, remove all doubt as to the building's function. The lobby doors are set back off the street, with entry made through El Paseo, a long Spanish arcade and open courtyard. The auditorium is a suprisingly small but beautifully arranged composition of false-front stucco villas roofed with vermilion tiles. The original proscenium arch (lost to Cinerama in 1955) represented a bridge between the two Spanish towns symbolized by the sidewall architecture. The original fire curtain (also gone) showed a river narrowing into the distance beneath the bridge. Copies of Catalan street lamps illuminate the two make-believe towns during the show.

When the Fox-Arlington opened, a portion of its tower housed a new nightspot for Santa Barbarans, El Club Chico. This cafe, perched on top of the lobby, offered its guest views both into the atmospheric auditorium and out over the more tangible buildings of Santa Barbara.

The Carthay Circle's art deco smooth, whitewashed exterior influenced the design of the Casino Building, with the Avalon Theatre (1929) tucked beneath the casino ballroom, in Avalon, California. Weber & Spaulding were commissioned by Phillip Wrigley, the chewing-gum king, to build the Casino as the central nightspot of Catalina Island, which the *Motion Picture Herald* pegged as "the not-too-private

fairyland of Mr. Wrigley." The Casino Building and its theater make up an appropriately playful centerpiece.

The underwater-inspired murals above the entry doors of the Avalon and the dark, curved lobby promenade evoke the feeling of a fantastic submarine adventure. The low walls of the theater's auditorium curve overhead, converging to form a soft, pink atmospheric dome. In place of the plaster that Eberson used to create his skies, Weber & Spaulding stretched two layers of heavy fabric across a rigid wooden frame. Along the side walls, murals depict scenes from the history of the island. Stylized antelopes, Indians, and Spanish monks populate the views. The image woven into the fire curtain, entitled "The Flight of Fancy Westward," shows two figures surfing on the crest of a wave, superimposed on a topographical map of Catalina Island. The *Motion Picture Herald* gave a tongue-in-cheek description of the artwork: ". . . an impressionistic representation of man unfettered amid a boundless Nature. It is allegory. It is history. And it may be hope. One assumes that it is also Catalina." Supervising this rose-colored dreamworld, a Botticellian Venus rises above the grillwork proscenium arch.

Among the first pure art deco theaters in California was the Fox-Wilshire (1930) in Los Angeles, by architect S. Charles Lee. The silver-and-black chevrons dominating the design were a popular art deco trademark. Lee's other art deco theaters include the Fox (1930, razed) in Phoenix, Arizona. The organ grills were silverleafed with gold highlights. A metallic sunburst spread across the ceiling from the radiating acoustic frames of the proscenium arch. A special feature of the Phoenix Fox was the row of street lights alongside the lobby staircase. The lights were set in spun silver balls on the end of fifteen-foot uprights.

A column-rimmed sculpture garden supplanted the conventional organ screens in the Southtown.

CARTHAY CIRCLE THEATRE

The art moderne Casino Building that houses the Avalon Theater (1929) rises out of the harbor alongside Catalina Island.

The street facade of the Fox (1932), *top left*, in Florence, California was mission movie house, with a Spanish-roofed porte-cochère. Under the arched entry, *bottom left*, was a vision of Old Spain; the box office was out of sight up the curving stairs.

A program cover from the Carthay Circle (1926) in Los Angeles. The Spanish tower against the night sky was a powerful advertisement for the theater.

The stage of the Fox-Wilshire (1930) in Los Angeles is framed in a metallic art deco meshwork.

The arches and towers along the south side of the Atlanta Fox (1929) give an Arabian flavor to the Georgia dusk.

Santa Barbara's most prominent landmark is the Arlington's Spanish Mission spire, *above*.

A California dusk envelopes the neon-trimmed, Mission-style Fox Riverside (1929), *left*.

The rose-colored atmospheric Avalon Theater (1929), *below*, is submerged beneath the ballroom floor of Catalina Island's Casino Building.

The arched bridge was lost in 1955 to wide-screen movies, but the vermilion-roofed haciendas still enclose the auditorium of the Fox-Arlington (1931) in Santa Barbara, California.

The glorious light-bulb marquee of the Warner (1931), *above*, in Erie, Pennsylvania, is one of the few golden-age marquees not replaced with a neon version.

Rapp & Rapp designed the Warner (1930), *right*, in West Chester, Pennsylvania, with a colorful and bizarre art deco look.

The symbolic columns in the Denver Paramount (1930), *top left*, including this one extended through the balcony, are capped by fan-shaped frosted-glass fixtures.

Rapp & Rapp's traditional French sidewall arrangement is beautifully translated into art deco inside the Paramount (1931), *left*, in Aurora, Illinois.

The vaulted grand lobby of the Hollywood Pantages (1930), *above*, is the wonderful exception to the hard-edged geometric forms decorating the rest of the theater.

B. Marcus Priteca astutely worked copper into the color scheme of Anaconda, Montana's art deco Washoe Theater (1936), *right*.

The Choral Steps, used on occasion by the Rockettes, extend the performance space halfway around the auditorium of New York's Radio City Music Hall (1932), *above*.

A familiar view, *left*, of Radio City's centerpiece, "The Showplace of the Nation."

The downstairs lounge of the Paramount (1931) in Oakland, California, is pure art deco, with matching carpet and couch. Just off this lounge is the Black Lacquer Room, designed originally as a women's smoking lounge.

*Facing page.* The art deco murals of the Phoenix Fox (1930) were ground to dust during the theater's demolition in 1975.

The classically inspired facade and foyer staircase of the Los Angeles Theater (1931) nearly match the grandeur of the San Francisco Fox—not quite as rich, but then S. Charles Lee did not have the Fox money to splurge.

Despite the decorative direction indicated by Lee's early art deco designs, his masterpiece was the last of the great traditional picture palaces. The predominant style of the Los Angeles Theater (1931) is French barococo just shy of the richness of Lamb's San Francisco Fox, built two years earlier. The wonderfully ostentatious foyer of the Los Angeles centers around a sweeping grand staircase. At the far end of the landing a tall mural "after Fragonard" serves as a backdrop for a twenty-foot fountain. Strings of crystal beads hang down the sides of the fountain to simulate sprays of water.

A polychrome plaster ceiling arches above the Los Angeles's auditorium. The focal point of the space is a three-dimensional fire curtain, depicting a collection of personages from the seventeenth-century French court. The figures are raised from the cloth backing in pillowy bas-relief. Overall the theater is an appropriate finale for traditional palace design.

The major palace architects did not abandon their habits when art deco began to dominate, but their designs lost much of their power with the stylistic changeover. Their traditional palatial schemes did not translate well into art

THE PALACE ARCHITECTS

In the theater's early years it was possible to relax in the Los Angeles's lower lounge and not miss the movie. A duplicate print of the feature was projected onto the small screen on the wall.

The house curtain of the Los Angeles Theater depicts French Royalty in a tapestrylike way.

John Eberson's art deco output includes the Rex Theater in Paris, a French-Moorish atmospheric with an art deco proscenium arch.

deco patterning. Without the marble columns, heavy drapes, and fine artwork, their later theaters lacked esthetic richness as well. John Eberson, no longer commissioned for atmospheric designs, suffered a similar loss of inspiration in the transition to art deco. Eberson's Penn Theatre (1935) in Washington's Capitol Hill district is functional but ordinary. Bland is the best word to characterize Lamb's design for the Warner (1931) in Torrington, Connecticut (although comparison with movie theaters built but a few years later make even the Warner look exciting). Lamb's best art deco theaters were built outside the United States for the Metro chain (a subsidiary of Metro-Goldwyn-Mayer), in South Africa, In-

dia, and Australia. Lamb also designed some wonderful art moderne exteriors, most notably for Greyhound bus stations in Detroit and New York (the 1936 station in front of the old Pennsylvania Station).

Among the major firms, Rapp & Rapp were most successful in making the stylistic switch. The first hints of art deco in their theater design are visible inside the St. Louis Ambassador (1928). The lobby is French palatial, but the auditorium walls are decorated with a flat stencilled design. Rapp & Rapp reversed this arrangement in the Milwaukee Warner (1929, now the Centre), with a French baroque auditorium fronted by a full-blown art deco lobby. The silver-backed mirrors along

the lobby walls are framed by shimmering silver arches in a tight geometric pattern.

The Warner (1930) in West Chester, Pennsylvania, is covered by a crazy quilt of art deco patterns. The flat-topped ceiling features a semiatmospheric mural, with jagged forms representing the symbols of the zodiac. A local writer referred to Rapp & Rapp's design as "a collossal composite of Renaissance, Greek, Mayan, French, Egyptian, even Finnish." Entertaining as the Warner is, its walls and ceiling look more than anything like a child's crayon scribble.

One of Rapp & Rapp's more important transitional theaters was the Warner (1931) in Erie, Pennsylvania.

Loew's took over operation of the Grand
Opera House (1896) in Atlanta in 1916,
but waited until 1932 to remodel.
Thomas Lamb then performed the
art deco facelift.

No longer French but not yet art deco, the
Ambassador (1928) in St. Louis is Rapp
& Rapp in transition.

The Paramount (1931) in Aurora, Illinois, is a surprising hybrid of French Renaissance and art deco that blossomed beautifully.

Under a latticework ceiling similar to that of the Brooklyn Paramount, Rapp & Rapp designed art deco versions of the baroque-inspired side bays in the Brooklyn theater. The blend of art deco and classical sensibility was what led to Rapp & Rapp's best art deco theater, the Paramount (1931) in Aurora, Illinois. The Paramount's auditorium is an ingenious art deco translation of the traditional picture palace. The side bays are filled with brightly colored canvas murals. The columns dividing the bays are actually flattened corrugated plaster pilasters topped by metallic ornamentation that is curled to give the appearance of Ionic capitals. Rapp & Rapp's

trademark sunburst is present as a spiky frosted-glass chandelier above the auditorium.

The plans of the Aurora Paramount must have been circulated in Paramount's offices throughout the country, because several near twins to the Aurora theater were built. These included Paramount theaters in Boston (1932) by A. W. Bowditch, Amarillo (1932) by W. Scott Dunne, and Denver (1930) by T. H. Buell, who had previously worked for Rapp & Rapp in Chicago.

The general acceptance of art deco in these designs signaled the end to movie theaters' being decorated in the styles

of royal palaces, whether European or Far Eastern. Despite this transition, the golden age was not over. The theaters built in the early 1930's were not only the clearest expression of art deco architecture in America, but also some of the most original among all the concoctions of the palace architects.

Rapp & Rapp remodeled Adler & Sullivan's Schiller Theater (1892) from a music hall into an art deco movie theater. The new brass doors in the carriage lobby were a mistake—customers had trouble figuring out how to open them.

Tribal masks blend in with the geometric art deco patterns along the arch and organ screens of the Paramount (1930) in Fort Wayne, Indiana.

# ART DECO GIANTS

As with art nouveau, the founders of art deco set out to devise a wholly new system of ornamentation drawn from nature. There were parallels between the two styles, but their philosophies differed significantly. The richly curvilinear, organic forms of art nouveau were designed in opposition to the sterility of early machine-age design. Art deco practitioners welcomed the new technology and assimilated mass-produced elements into their ornamentation, as exemplified by the decorations on the setbacks of New York's Chrysler Building. The naturalistic forms in art deco designs were organized in zigzag geometrical patterns, and built from a range of materials, including aluminum, chrome, and, the old standby, plaster.

The first great art deco movie palace was the Hollywood Pantages (1930), built on the corner of the famous intersection of Hollywood and Vine. The theater was the work of B. Marcus Priteca, who was still dreaming up new designs for Alex Pantages. For the Hollywood Pantages, Priteca used what he felt was "an original treatment that would best exemplify America of the moment . . . motifs that were modern, never futuristic—based on time-tested classicism of enduring good taste and beauty."

The classical origins are difficult to track down, but it's hard to imagine anyone really caring once the glorious geometry of the overall scheme has been witnessed. This treatment extends from the columns of the front facade to the mirrors of the women's lounge. The jarring diagonals of the auditorium ceiling are a marked contrast to the organic curvature of the barrel vault over the grand lobby. There are a few statues along the staircases at either end, but these figures are unlike any classical statuary: in matching sets for the two

staircases, the golden statues represent an aviatrix with goggles and scarf and a Hollywood director crouching behind a hard-working cameraman. With its bold art deco lines and prime location, the Pantages was the site of many gala premieres.

In 1931, Priteca designed another unusual art deco theater, for Anaconda, a small town in Montana. The Depression forced a delay in construction, and the Washoe Theater finally opened in 1936. It was well worth the wait. Because of the delay, the Washoe gained the distinction of being the last movie palace of the golden age. Fittingly, Anaconda is no larger than Baraboo, Wisconsin, the site, sixteen years earlier, of the first movie palace.

Anaconda's history as an important copper-mining town is reflected by Priteca's design, most notably in the copper organ screens and the metallic ram's-head medallions ringing the auditorium ceiling. The pastel ceiling surrounds an allegorical mural with sketches drawn to symbolize the world's dependence on copper. The beautiful composition of the auditorium is set off by a royal blue silk stage curtain with a pair of elks woven at the center.

Priteca's West Coast colleague, G. Albert Lansburgh, ended his career as a palace architect with the Los Angeles Warner's Western Theater (1931). Closed in 1932 and reopened in 1936 as the Wiltern, its bright green-

Opening night at the Hollywood Pantages, June 4, 1930, with klieg lights crisscrossing the sky.

Inside the auditorium of the Hollywood Pantages, B. Marcus Priteca completely transformed his classical model into wonderfully abstract geometric ornaments.

and-gold lobby is an elliptical art deco version of the Garden of Eden. A golden railing curves around the second-level promenade. Inside the auditorium, a huge meshwork fan spreads across the ceiling.

With 3,408 seats, the Oakland Paramount (1931) is the largest art deco palace ever built on the West Coast. Architect Timothy L. Pflueger had built two picture palaces across the bay in San Francisco—the Spanish baroque Castro Theater (1922) and the Moorish Alhambra Theater (1925). Pflueger first used art deco in the Tulare Theater

(1928) in Tulare, California. The theater resembles a back-lot desert fortress, thus earning its tag "Fox Foreign Legion." In place of the stud lighting used on the exteriors of the older movie theaters, the facade of the Tulare is outlined in glowing neon, a medium that had been introduced to the United States only five years before.

Unlike Pflueger's earlier theaters, the Oakland Paramount is pure art deco. Parts of the decorative scheme viewed individually may appear gaudy and overworked—the golden girls lining the walls of the grand foyer and the

A wispy mural engulfs a circular mirror on a lobby wall inside the Washoe.

The Washoe Theater (1936) in Anaconda, Montana, is an art deco shrine to the copper-based economy of the Big Sky country.

THE PALACE ARCHITECTS

The celebrities arriving for the opening of
the Western (1931) made their grand entrances across the Bridge of Stars. Warner
Brothers built the bridge across Wilshire
Boulevard and decorated it with electric
flowers just for the occasion.

A plaster tent forms the auditorium ceiling of San Francisco's Castro Theater
(1922).

The neon trim of the Tulare Theater (1928) in Tulare, California, is art deco's answer to the stud-lighted fronts of earlier movie theaters.

An illuminated grillwork serves as a symbolic rain forest above the grand foyer of the Paramount (1931) in Oakland, California.

scenes of primitive Eden on the auditorium side walls—but the overall design is an art deco masterpiece.

Pflueger followed the art deco creed of seeking to integrate technology and art into an ideal architectural style. All services were incorporated into the building's structure. The unending variety of lighting fixtures are all incorporated into the decoration, with some completely hidden from view. Inside the foyer, above the entry doors, seven panes of sand-blasted translucent glass are magically transformed by hidden lights into the glowing yellow Fountain of Light. The foyer ceiling is hidden above a suspended metal grillwork. The zigzag geometrical patterning of the grill is a jazz-age composition, illuminated in green, transporting patrons to a lush tropical jungle.

Inside the auditorium, the Columns of Incandescence frame the stage. The columns appear to be made of frosted glass but are actually an aluminum alloy lighted from behind. Neptune rises out of the proscenium arch to dominate the golden plasterwork sounding board. Here the plaster yields to another ceiling grill. The romantic vision outlined by the grill's metal frame can be made to glow in a rainbow of colors. This Canopy of Light over the auditorium and the metallic imitation rain forest above the foyer also serve as ventilation ducts. Overall, the secret of the Paramount's glory was Pflueger's ability to camouflage all the

A full 6,000 stand at attention at the start of a benefit performance held during World War II inside New York's Radio City Music Hall (1932).

*Facing page.* The Fountain of Light inside the Oakland Paramount takes on a dreamlike character in this view, with workers moving among the glass panels.

A view of the Rockettes never seen by the general public—seated in the Music Hall on a break.

*Facing page.* The stairs from the Music Hall's grand foyer rise in tandem with the figures painted on the wall above in Ezra Winter's Mural.

mechanical operation of the building with art deco glitter.

The largest movie theater ever built was the last of the big-city art deco palaces, New York's Radio City Music Hall (1932). Roxy abandoned the theater that bore his name to manage the Music Hall. The theater seats 5,960, more than any other movie palace, but Roxy advertised its capacity as 6,000-plus. (He counted every seat in the building proper, including the chairs in the orchestra pit and the stools for the elevator operators.)

Radio City Music Hall's most memorable sight has always been the glowing, golden arches framing the stage. The arches soar overhead above the main floor in a gesture as elegant as it is offhanded. Legend places the original inspiration for this arrangement

with Roxy himself. The bands of fluted plaster are said to symbolize a golden sunset Roxy once experienced from the deck of an ocean liner.

Roxy's other major contribution to the Music Hall was the theater's hallmark act, the Rockettes. The dance team has its origins with the sixteen Missouri Rockets, who first kicked their heels in St. Louis during 1925. In 1927 the act doubled in size and was renamed the Roxyettes when the team moved to the Roxy Theatre in New York. Roxy brought them with him when he moved to Radio City. A legal battle between the Music Hall and the Roxy lead to the final name change.

With a new show to put on every week, the first Rockettes were constantly rehearsing. Only one backstage rehearsal hall is big enough for all

thirty-six to kick at the same time. Gyms and dormitories were built on top of the theater for the Rockettes. Publicity photos from the thirties show the Rockettes playing shuffleboard on the roof of Rockefeller Center or resting in the dorms, but most of their days were spent in rehearsal developing their renowned dancing precision.

The assortment of technical devices used to put on a show at the Music Hall is staggering. The three stage elevators are powered by the same type of hydraulic system used on aircraft carriers during World War II. The stage curtain, weighing over three tons, can be raised and lowered in a variety of patterns by thirteen motor-driven metal cables. The cables are controlled by an operator seated before a brass board that looks like something from the wheelhouse of a yacht. In another part of the backstage control center are valves that can release a misty curtain of steam from a line of vents across the entire 140 feet of the stage opening.

The Music Hall is part of Rockefeller Center, a complex that was the work of a team of architectural firms. Despite the design-by-committee approach, Rockefeller Center is a coherent package of buildings on a colossal scale, a major landmark in midtown Manhattan.

Donald Deskey was the chief designer of Radio City Music Hall. Deskey planned a silver-and-black art deco design for the grand foyer but was overruled by John D. Rockefeller, who wanted warmer tones in this grand hall. Deskey complied by transferring his preferred color scheme to the lower lobby and designing a new main lobby in brown, beige, and gold. The curving staircase leading up from the grand foyer has as a backdrop a mural by Ezra Winter. At sixty by forty feet, it is so large it had to be painted on an abandoned tennis court and transported in sections to the Music Hall.

The combination of highly original ornamentation and technical wizardry in the design of a theater set at the heart of a huge commercial complex should strike a familiar chord for theater historians. The golden acoustic arches of the Auditorium Theatre (1889) in Chicago are only its most visible similarity to Radio City Music Hall. The two theaters have much in common—advanced stage machinery, huge seating capacities spread across several levels, and unique ornamentation. The buildings that house these two theaters are both significant in the history of America's urban architecture. The world had changed drastically over the years separating construction of the two theaters, but they represent the beginning and end of the same age. The tiny Washoe Theater in Anaconda, Montana, notwithstanding, completion of Radio City Music Hall marked the close of the golden age of movie palaces. The glories of that age would have been impossible without the brilliant concepts first introduced by Adler & Sullivan's Auditorium Building, a structure Frank Lloyd Wright said, with remarkable prescience, was "fifty years ahead of its time."

# ART DECO IN DECLINE

The Roaring Twenties have been characterized as an age of frivolity and naive optimism, an image the movies and movie palaces helped create. Under the burden of the Depression, America simmered down and the golden age of palace design reached its end. Art deco had been adopted as an economy measure of sorts, an attempt to maintain a richness of design without spending quite so much. The art deco theaters were more severe in their ornament and less expensive, using more plaster and mirrors than the traditional palaces with their marble, crystal, and antiques. The size and ornamental variety of the largest art deco palaces extended the spirit of the golden age into the Depression years, but the trends in theater design were clearly set for smallness and simplicity

R. C. Reamer, the architect of Seattle's Fifth Avenue Theater, built the Fox (1931) in Spokane. Underwater murals recall what might be called the aquarium deco of the Avalon on Catalina Island, but the Fox lacks the spatial appeal of the Avalon. The lobbies and the auditorium of the Fox are flat and boxy.

Art deco degenerated further in the theaters built in the years following. The most popular decorative element of the period was a convoluted stretch of gold plaster, variously referred to as feathers or curling waves. Bright neon, colored fabrics, and these applied golden featers are the only items of note in theaters of the Depression (e.g., the Sacramento Crest, the Centre in Denver, and the Fox-Westwood Village in Los Angeles).

A few art moderne curves enliven the interior of the Chicago Esquire (1937), by Pereira & Pereira. The *Encyclopedia Britannica* printed a picture of

The neon icing is the only architectural flourish of note at Dallas's Inwood Theater (1941). By this time the movie palaces of the previous decades were considered overembellished and extravagant.

This doctored, "atmospheric" photograph of the Chicago Esquire (1937) was used in the *Encyclopedia Britannica* to illustrate the ideal modern theater. Cosmetic surgery removed the large building next door from the photograph, replacing it with a cloud-streaked sky.

*Facing page.* The title on the Paramount's marquee appears to tell the story for this pair among the crowd on Times Square.

the main facade of the Esquire, lauding the overall design as the ideal movie theater, with its clean lines and simplicity of operation. Clearly tastes had changed. No longer did moviegoers expect a royal welcome from doormen, ushers, and lounge attendants. The architectural treatments of movie palaces were now considered overexuberant, if not downright wasteful.

Contrary to popular belief, movie attendance declined during the Depression, rebounding only during World War II. The movies shared a postwar boom with babies, but the theaters built during the late forties were unexceptional. The Rapp brothers and Eberson continued to build theaters through the forties and fifties, but the money was no longer there to build the old-style palaces, and the times had changed. The clinching blow came with the antitrust actions in 1948. The studios had formerly been able to give their theater chains exclusive rights to the first run of their best pictures. With

the studios debarred from film exhibition, investment dollars were in short supply. The art of theater design steadily declined, reaching its nadir in the 1960s with the small shopping-mall movie houses. Located along the omnipresent commercial strips radiating out from the cities, these theaters contain little more than seats, screens, and candy counters inside their shoebox forms. Yet the success of the mall cinemas was sufficient to drive many downtown palaces out of business.

The downtown movie palaces had been in trouble since 1950. Theater owners underestimated the power of television. Not even Cinerama or 3-D could stem the tide. The flight of affluent city dwellers to the suburbs was the last nail in the coffin for the downtown theaters. The shopping-center cinemas were closer at hand, parking was easier, and the lots were safer than most city streets. The golden age of the movie palaces had been supplanted by the dark age.

# LOST AND FOUND

# 3

## PAVED INTO OBLIVION

The first theater to go was the Paradise in Chicago. For all its glory, Eberson's theater appears to have been jinxed from the start. After a number of theater operators had abandoned the project, Balaban & Katz took over final construction of the Paradise in 1928. Their aim was to compete with the Marbro, the Marks Brothers' flagship theater, built the year before just a few blocks from the Paradise. Superior booking at the Paradise combined with the Depression to drive the Marks Brothers under. B & K took over the Marbro in 1930 and moved their top shows into that house because it had a larger capacity than the Paradise. Unable to compete with the theater it once bested, the Paradise was slated for demolition in 1954.

The theater put up a valiant fight. Although the blueprints showed the supporting beams and posts of the balcony to be twelve inches thick, the actual dimensions were often as much as three times those shown. It took two companies two years to bring down the Paradise. The first company went bankrupt, its owner driven to suicide. It was a sad and messy end for a bewitchingly beautiful theater. The Marbro, Levy & Klein's finest theater, was pounded to rubble a few years later.

The list of theaters demolished during the 1960s is long and heartbreaking. It includes some of the best work the palace architects ever did. Just as *The Best Remaining Seats*, Ben Hall's gala scrapbook of the golden age, was going to press in 1961, his favorite theater, the Roxy, was being razed. Major work by nearly every one of the palace architects was among subsequent casualties. Hoffman & Henon built a half dozen theaters in Philadelphia; all, including their magnificent Mastbaum, have vanished over the past twenty years. Rapp & Rapp's Times Square Paramount was gutted and removed from the interior of the Paramount Building. Thomas Lamb's last major palace, the eerily Oriental atmospheric Loew's 72nd Street, was torn down in 1961 when it was only twenty-nine years old. Lamb's Cincinnati Albee, with its supremely elegant grand foyer, fell victim to Fountain Square development schemes. A failed bond issue sealed the fate of San Francisco's Fox, a theater many considered not only Lamb's best, but also the most palatial theater ever built.

Often these theaters were demolished to make way for yet another office block, hotel, or, that menace of all historic structures, a parking lot. In one of the most absurd transformations on record, the interior of the Michigan Theater (1926) in Detroit was partially gutted and converted into a parking garage. An auto ramp now runs through Rapp & Rapp's palatial foyer. The fragmented plaster of the ceiling coves and the proscenium arch loom above the third parking level. Inexplicably, the movie screen remains in place,

The exterior of the Chicago Paradise possessed the stately grandeur of a French palace as well as a magical marquee.

The ultimate architectural insult—the Michigan Theatre (1926) in Detroit was mortally wounded by its conversion to a parking garage.

giving the former theater the appearance of the world's first triple-decker drive-in.

If so, it would not be the only instance of theaters stacked one on another. Several theaters across the country have been piggybacked, with a separate auditorium created in the balcony by walling it off from the main floor. The origin of this setup dates back to turn-of-the-century roof-garden theaters and some intentionally planned double-deckers. First among the latter was Lamb's Wintergarden (1914), built above the Loew's Yonge Street Theater in Toronto. In Balti-

more, John Eberson inserted a Spanish atmospheric, patrolled by ushers in bullfighter costumes, into a ballroom above an older theater. The Baltimore Valencia (1926) was perched on top of the expansive Century Theater, designed and built five years earlier by John J. Zink. A popular joke around town in 1926 was that, paradoxically, the Valencia was both the newest and oldest theater in the city (because it was "over a century").

The division of large theaters into several smaller theaters has been another curse, with additional screens set up in the manner of contemporary

multicinemas. The Bronx Paradise was twinned and then triplexed, destroying its atmospheric quality. The tiny Holland Theater in Bellefontaine, Ohio, was chopped into six separate theaters. The owners of the Midland in Kansas City wisely kept the theater's palatial auditorium intact, instead converting an old screening room and a downstairs lounge into additional theaters.

The size and location of the surviving palaces have worked against them in a changing real-estate market. In the big cities, only a few of the larger picture palaces still show first-run films. Theater operators in the past decade

found that desperate measures were called for to save the last theaters of the golden age. If the new movies could not sell enough tickets to fill the huge movie houses, something else was needed to draw the crowds.

The grand lobby contains an auto ramp. The auditorium's remaining plasterwork hangs suspended, like a cutaway model.

The former St. Louis Theater (1926) enjoys a second life as Powell Hall.

# AN END TO THE SLAUGHTER

The story would soon become a familiar one across the country, but the path to salvation for the old St. Louis Theater was a wonderfully original inspiration. The 1926 Rapp & Rapp Louis XIV–style theater had, like most downtown palaces, fallen on hard times by the 1960s. Coincidentally, the well-established St. Louis Symphony Orchestra was searching for a new home. Through an admirable blend of historical hindsight and economic foresight, a plan was developed for converting the old movie theater into a "new" symphony hall. Fittingly, the film *The Sound of Music* ended the St. Louis's days as a picture palace in 1966. The theater opened as a music hall two years later, rechristened Powell Hall.

The high-quality acoustical potential of the movie palaces for symphonic production was first demonstrated to the public at large by Eugene Ormandy

in 1940 during a concert he conducted in Philadelphia's Mastbaum Theater. (Ormandy had begun his career as the conductor of the house orchestra of New York's Capitol Theater in the 1920s.)

The particular suitability of Rapp & Rapp's work for this kind of conversion became apparent in the years after Powell Hall opened. The firm's theaters in Pittsburgh, Omaha, and Youngstown, Ohio, followed the lead set by the St. Louis. Of these three later conversions, only the Omaha Orpheum (1927) is a faithful restoration of the Rapp brothers' original decor. The Youngstown Warner (1931, now Power Hall) still has a few bits and pieces of the side-wall decorations visible between the new acoustical panels set inside the organ screens and side bays. A particularly large sound baffle shaped like a sand dollar was placed

within the rim of the auditorium's ceiling dome.

Pittsburgh's new Heinz Hall was created in 1971 through the wholesale conversion of the Loew's Penn Theater (1927). Some stencil designs painted where the organ screen once stood and a ring of bull's-eye coves around the ceiling dome are all that remain to remind us of Heinz Hall's past as a movie theater. The Loew's Penn was the first Pittsburgh palace to show talkies, but with the conversion it appears to have stepped back into an earlier age. The

The auditorium of the Omaha Orpheum (1927) is Rapp & Rapp's economy French treatment, but the local symphony found that even the firm's less extravagant theaters are attractive and acoustically sound.

Drastic alterations transformed the Loew's Penn (1927), *above*, from a movie palace into Heinz Hall, *top of page* 193, the stately new home of the Pittsburgh Symphony Orchestra.

new theater is fully a nineteenth-century music hall, complete with the traditional red, white, and gold color scheme.

Symphonies in Oakland, Columbus, and Vancouver, British Columbia, chose the restoration route to find new homes in run-down picture palaces. The city arts council renovated the Vancouver Orpheum, built by B. Marcus Priteca in 1927. Anthony B. Heinsbergen, Priteca's chief decorator from 1916 to 1928, returned to

Vancouver in 1977 to design a new mural for the ceiling dome. A new, permanently fixed bandshell was installed on stage, decorated with vault lines closely modeled after those rimming the ceiling of the auditorium proper.

When the Oakland Symphony reopened the Paramount in 1972, every detail of the original 1931 art deco extravagance had been painstakingly restored. The grime was stripped from the glass panels of the Fountain of

Red lights blend in with yellow, turning one panel of the Oakland Paramount's ceiling grill (*below*) into a giant Valentine's Day card. Even without the rainbow effect, the grill creates a spectacular canopy for the art deco auditorium.

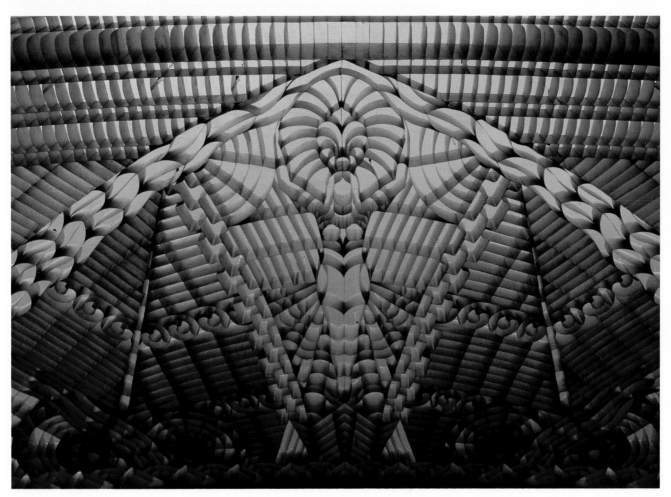

Renderings of a pair of lost giants from the golden age:
Hoffman & Henon's Mastbaum (1929) in Philadelphia and
W. W. Ahlschlager's Roxy (1927) in New York.

Sound baffles fill the organ screen of Power Hall (1931, formerly the Warner) in Youngstown, Ohio.

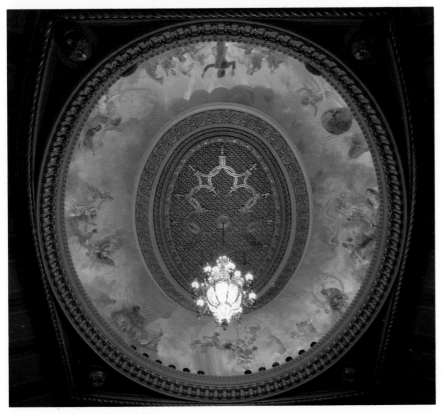

When the local symphony moved into the Orpheum (1927) in Vancouver, British Columbia, artist A. B. Heinsbergen was commissioned to redesign the ceiling mural he had painted fifty years earlier.

The crutches of the healed line the lobby walls of the former Loew's Valencia (1929) in Queens, New York, now a church.

The original color scheme of the Loew's Valencia, *above right*, was quite subdued for an Eberson theater. The new owners, the Pentecostal Church, gave the theater's walls a more exotic paint job, *right*, put a pulpit on stage, and hung a chandelier from the plaster sky.

Gymnasts and basketball players are the
star performers inside the former
Brooklyn Paramount (1928).

As the Bismarck Pavilion, *above*, the former Palace Theater (1926) handles some of Chicago's convention trade.

Jack McGovern's Music Hall, *above right*, promotes nightclub acts on the stage of the former Seattle Fox (1929).

The best known among the four murals which James Daugherty painted in the lobby of Cleveland's Loew's State Theater (1921) is "The Spirit of Cinema—America," *right*. It was once featured on the cover of *Life* magazine.

*Facing page.*
A restaurant has been installed beneath the rotunda of the Allen Theater (1922), *top left*, in Cleveland.

A bulbous onion dome, *top right*, in central Beverly Hills marks the location of the former Beverly Theater (1925). The new boutique, *bottom*, matches the glitter of the old theater's flashy elephant murals.

Sidewalk graphics and umbrella canopies decorate the entrances to Heinz Hall. The doors were added during the conversion, after the arched entry to the theater had been sealed with glass panels.

*Facing page.* The considerably altered interior of Los Angeles's former Pantages Theater (1921): jewelry merchants rule the main floor, fur displays fill the organ screens, and a glittery chandelier hangs from the ceiling dome.

One of the cleanup duties when the Oakland Paramount (1931) was renovated in 1973 was a thorough vacuuming of the ceiling grills above the auditorium and foyer.

Light, and the ceiling grills were vacuumed. A computer print-out was used to reproduce the colors and patterns of the original carpeting. The Paramount Theatre of the Arts stands as the gaudiest orchestra hall in the country, and one of the most glamorous.

Officials at the Ohio Theatre (1928) in Columbus chose piecemeal restoration, with the major work spread over the course of a decade.

They also chose to institute a policy to permit rental of the theater when it was not in use by the symphony. More than any other single case, the continued success of the Ohio served to revive interest in the movie palaces, prompting dozens of cities across the country to save their theaters. Reflecting the value of the effort in Columbus, the Ohio Theatre was designated a National Historic Landmark in 1978.

# THE RESCUE CONTINUES

Public bond issues, local arts committees, private enterprise—the forces behind movie-palace reclamation projects have been as diverse as their new uses. The great majority of these converted performing-arts centers are truly multipurpose, hosting a variety of stage acts, civic functions, and occasionally even movies.

One of the most significant rescue operations was organized in Cleveland, where three neighboring theater renovations have been joined to form the revitalized Playhouse Square. The three movie houses fit snugly together like pieces of a jigsaw puzzle. In a competitive move against B. F. Keith's Palace Theater (1922), still on the drawing boards of Rapp & Rapp in 1920, Marcus Loew bought all the property to the side and rear of the Palace's corner site. By designing two of the world's longest lobbies, Loew's architect Thomas Lamb was able to wrap both the Loew's Ohio (1921) and the Loew's State (1921) around the spot where the Palace would be built. Fifty years later, plans were set in motion to put on intimate stage productions in both the lobby of the Loew's State and the grand hall of the Palace. These shows' suc-

Intimate theater performances in the lobbies of Cleveland's downtown picture palaces have helped foot the bill for renovation. Cabaret acts are staged in the formal French reception lobby of the Palace Theater (1922), *below*. Thomas Lamb's Adamesque lobby of the State Theater (1921), *overleaf*, serves as a dinner theater.

cesses subsequently helped draw the crowds back to the reconstructed downtown section, and funds began to flow in for the full renovation of the auditoriums for live performance.

Cleveland is one of more than a hundred cities that have counted on theater-reuse projects to bring suburbanites back downtown at night. Downtown mall developments, an urban phenomenon of the 1970s, have been anchored by these rehabilitated theaters in many cities. These include theaters as diverse as the Second Empire Grand Opera House (1871) in Wilmington, Delaware, and the art deco Paramount (1931) in Aurora, Illinois.

At times the focus of renovation has narrowed or shifted. Following extensive interor modifications, the Wells Theatre (1913) in Norfolk, Virginia, became home to the Virginia Stage Company. Providence's Trinity Square Repertory Company converted the Majestic, a 1917 vaudeville house, into the piggybacked Lederer Theatre. In doing so, they saved the glass-domed lobby rotunda while inserting a concrete slab at midlevel in the old auditorium to create two smaller theaters in a contemporary design.

Subdivision met with considerable opposition when it was planned in 1979 for the auditorium of the Indiana

Theater (1927) in Indianapolis. The chief attraction of Rubush & Hunter's original design was the richly detailed plaster decoration of the auditorium walls, matched only by similar treatment of the terra-cotta facade. Developers wanted to keep the facade intact, but total gutting was planned for the auditorium. An organization calling itself STOP (Save The Ornamental Plaster) finally convinced them to retain much of the interior plasterwork, and the playhouse was converted.

Old and new theaters were joined in 1980 to form the Civic Center of Madison, Wisconsin. The former Capitol Theater (1928), an economy

Ruffled East Indian ornaments coat the
main facade and auditorium walls of
Rubush & Hunter's Indiana Theater
(1927) in Indianapolis.

model Rapp & Rapp French design, was restored and renamed the Oscar Meyer Theatre. The neighboring Montgomery-Ward Building was gutted and redesigned as an art gallery. The contemporary-style Isthmus Playhouse was built alongside the triangle of space joining the two older bulidngs. The net result is an effective and attractive arts complex at a fraction of the cost of a new facility.

Tables now fill the orchestra floors of the Uptown in Kansas City, Missouri, the United Artists in Louisville, and the St. Louis Ambassador, all built in 1928. As of 1980, these three theaters were being converted into dinner theaters. Low-hanging chandeliers, booths along the walls, and a terraced main floor have altered the movie-palace character of the Seattle Fox (1929). Las Vegas–style cabaret acts now rule the stage of the theater, reincarnated as Jack McGovern's Music Hall. (Detroit's Michigan Theater offered similar fare before its auditorium gave way to a parking garage.) A terraced main floor helped convert the auditorium of the Rapp & Rapp Palace Theater (1926) in Chicago into a banquet hall, serving the city's heavy convention business.

Most of the renovated movie palaces fall under the general heading of

The transformation of Chicago's Palace Theater (1926), *above*, from movie hall to banquet hall helped save both the theater and the adjacent hotel from demolition.

*Facing page.* Booths and tables have replaced the orchestra seats of the Seattle Fox (1929), now Jack McGovern's Music Hall. Chandeliers now hang from the coffered sounding board.

Decorative ornaments radiate in bands from the stage of the Loew's State (1928), now the Ocean State Performing Arts Center in Providence, Rhode Island.

Thomas Lamb's side wall colonnades of Keith's Memorial (1928) in Boston possess an exceptional elegance that even Rapp & Rapp must have envied.

performing-arts center. Recovery from economic ill health has often been difficult for these theaters, particularly in smaller cities and towns. Despite its quiet formal splendor, Rapp & Rapp's Loew's State Theater (1928) literally exploded on the Providence theater scene when it was built: a few months before the opening, one of the theater's electrical transformers blew up, blacking out the entire state of Rhode Island. A bright red-and-green macaw, the Loew's mascot, joined seven successive full house crowds for the opening film, William Haines in *Excess Baggage.* Ironically, that title came to reflect the status accorded the Loew's State by the

city in the early 1970s. By the end of the decade, with a mixture of symphony, ballet, and legitimate theater, the Loew's State found new life as the Ocean State Performing Arts Center.

Finding an appropriate entertainment identity has often been the greatest obstacle for theater-reuse projects. In 1978, W. Scott Dunne's Paramount Theater (1927) in Abilene, Texas, built as a comfortable Spanish atmospheric, was reborn as the Paramount Opry. Several palaces, notably the Atlanta Fox, cater mostly to rock shows. (Again, Detroit set the precedent, with many of Motown's greatest hits first sung live on the stage of the Fox.)

One of the most celebrated conversions serves to cement the stylistic and functional bonds that exist between the movie palaces and Old World theaters. Keith's Memorial (1928, now the Savoy) in Boston is a splendid stylistic hybrid designed by Thomas Lamb. The column-lined auditorium is a blend of Rapp & Rapp's French palatial with Lamb's barococo magnificence. Shortly after the theater turned fifty, it became the home of Sarah Caldwell's Opera Company of Boston. It was a marriage of music and architecture made in heaven, with a choir any angel would be proud to join.

# TRANSFORMATIONS 1: RELIGIOUS TIES

Not for nothing was New York's Roxy Theatre billed as "The Cathedral of the Motion Picture." W. W. Ahlschlager's ornamentation might have looked more appropriate in Vatican City than along Seventh Avenue. For the theater's inaugural evening, Roxy staged his own version of the Creation, complete with a solitary monk intoning, "Let there be light!" (A theater reviewer for *The New Yorker* appended, "And, by golly, there was light.")

Many of the palace architects drew inspiration from religious architecture. The cave-Gothic of C. Howard Crane's three United Artists theaters evoke a kind of religious reverence. Rapp & Rapp often looked to French and German baroque chapels for divine guidance. Levy & Klein's early designs for local synagogues were the major reason the firm was hired to design theaters for the Marks Brothers in Chicago.

The combination of Spanish and art deco popularized by the Fox–West Coast chain of theaters evolved from California's historic missions. From the outside, S. Charles Lee's Tower

Theater (1927) in Los Angeles looks more like a church than a theater, despite the loss of half its clock tower in an earthquake. Inside, only the plush seats in place of pews distinguish the auditorium from the interior of a church.

For all the stylistic similarities the movie palaces share with cathedrals and churches, it is doubtful that the palace architects envisioned what their religious trappings would lead to. Various religious groups have joined in the effort to save the remaining palaces, and their adaptive reuse has created some fairly unusual churches.

Three of Thomas Lamb's movie palaces in New York have been transformed into religious halls, including his landmark Regent Theater (1913). The Loew's Pitkin, a 1929 Lamb atmospheric, served for ten years as the Hudson Temple Cathedral before closing in the late 1970s. In 1969 the Loew's 175th Street Theater became the home of the United Church, with Frederick Eikerenkoetter (better known as Reverend Ike) in the pulpit. The fully refurbished interior glows

with a golden brilliance. The theater's exterior is more or less intact, with an unanticipated addition—Reverend Ike's prayer tower has been perched on the 176th Street side of the roof.

Another of the Loew's wonder theaters, the Spanish atmospheric Valencia (1929) of John Eberson, has been converted for religious use. In 1977 the Loew's Corporation donated Queens's finest movie palace to the Pentecostal Church, which converted the auditorium to their Tabernacle of Prayer for All People. The crutches of the healed hang along a wall in the lobby, and a new color scheme heightens the gaudiness inherent in any Eberson design. A great deal of furor arose in some circles when parishioners decided to hang a massive chandelier from the center of the blue plaster sky. A less obtrusive operation was performed on Eberson's statuary, as described by the church's presiding Reverend Washington: "We covered the naked ladies up there. We put wings on them and they are angels. That one on the left, though, she has a miniskirt."

The Loew's Pitkin (1929) in Brooklyn, New York, with the organ and orchestra pit at stage level. After a few years as a church, the theater closed in 1970.

Chicago-based architect J. E. O. Pridmore placed a high-relief plaster frieze around the rim of the mock-tented ceiling of the Sheridan Theater (1927) in Chicago. The theater served temporarily as a synagogue in the seventies.

The artistically done draping job looks almost deliberate; John Eberson probably would have approved.

Eberson once described the Chicago Avalon (1927) as a place "where the royal nabobs and lords gather to exchange everything from fruit to human souls." Since 1970, when the theater became the Miracle Temple, human souls have been the prime concern of the former theater's new

owners. Even with the sky painted a gleaming silver and hung with fluorescent lights, much of the flavor of the original Middle Eastern design remains. Perhaps it was no accident that the Avalon, one of Eberson's most faithful adaptations, was designed to resemble a mosque.

Conversions to churches have proven just as popular in the Los Angeles area. These include the Belasco Theater (1926), designed by Morgan, Walls & Clements the year before they built the Mayan next door. The Mayan has been showing porno movies since its fiftieth birthday in 1977, while the Belasco has become home to the Metropolitan Church, a homosexual religious organization.

The Loyola and the Academy, two of S. Charles Lee's late art deco theaters in the Inglewood district of Los An-

geles, have been turned into churches. The Academy was built toward the end of the thirties in an art moderne style similar to that of the Pan Pacific Auditorium in Los Angeles. The Loyola, with its mid-1930s neoexpressionist swan-shaped exterior, was taken over by an Eastern religious group.

During the years when the palaces were being built, such conversions occasionally worked in reverse. Two stone churches built in the nineteenth century were transformed to theaters during the golden age. The Vita-Temple in Toledo, Ohio, was built in 1862 as the First Congregational Church. During the 1880s and 1890s, the building underwent something of an identity crisis, serving first as a combination dance floor and roller rink, and later as a billiard parlor. In the early 1900s it became the Temple Theater, a

The swan-shaped Loyola Theater in Inglewood, California, has become home for
the followers of Maharaji, a popular Eastern religious figure.

Arched stained-glass windows, retained
from the Toledo, Ohio, Vita-Temple's
years as a church, were partially blocked
by the theater marquee installed in 1928.
Fire destroyed the building five years later.

Boston's nineteenth-century Spiritualist Temple has survived as a moviehouse, the Exeter Street Theater (1914).

vaudeville hall. One of the first talking pictures, Al Jolson's *The Singing Fool* (with Vitaphone sound), started the theater, now the Vita-Temple, on its final career as a movie house in 1928. In what may have been an act of divine retribution for all these proceedings, the Vita-Temple burned to the ground in a spectacular blaze during the winter of 1933.

Since 1914 the Exeter Street Theatre in Boston has been housed within the former home of the Spiritualist Temple. The heavy brown stone building was designed by the firm of Hartwell & Richardson. The firm's junior partner was a disciple but not a relative of H. H. Richardson, the architect of the landmark Trinity Church just a few blocks away.

# TRANSFORMATIONS 2: ATHLETIC CONVERSIONS

When the Cincinnati YMCA moved to new quarters in the mid-twenties, the Shubert organization converted the old YMCA building into a theater by constructing seats above an old running track and spanning the pool with a wooden stage. All went well until a circus arrived in town for a show. The troupe's elephant ended up in an unscheduled cannonball dive into the former pool.

In Baltimore, a Swiss chalet–styled brick bathhouse, the 1870 Natatorium, ended its first century as a movie house. Converted in 1890 to the Howard Auditorium, a legitimate theater, the building received extensive remodeling and a new facade in 1903. As of 1941, the Howard became the Mayfair, a full-time movie house.

These inverted examples serve as early precedents for a number of adaptive reuse projects with athletic ends. Even the famous Chicago Auditorium has not been immune to such plans, if only temporarily. In the autumn of 1930, the newspapers announced the impending conversion of the Auditorium into two miniature-golf courses: "...one of six holes in the foyer and one of 18 on the main floor...on the stage will be erected a stucco replica of a country clubhouse with veranda, and background of artificial trees, privet hedge, and greensward, where hot dogs, pop, and lemonade may be purchased." For whatever reasons, this painful transition to "Lilliput golf" was never accomplished. During World War II, however, the USO did set up bowling alleys on the stage, but these were removed at the end of the war.

Bowling has been a popular choice for theater reuse. Eberson's Riviera (1927) in Omaha once had bowling alleys built above the orchestra seats. Hoffman & Henon's Spanish atmospheric Warner (1929, later Warren, razed) in Atlantic City and Ahlschlager's Chicago Belmont (1926) were

both redone as bowling alleys. For a change of pace, three late-1930s theaters—the Columbia in St. Louis, the Harbor Theater in Brooklyn, and the Belmont Shores in Long Beach, California—were totally gutted and racquetball courts were constructed in the former auditoriums.

The most startling of the athletic conversions occurred when Long Island University took over the 1928 Rapp & Rapp Brooklyn Paramount.

The grand lobby, an ersatz Hall of Mirrors, was transformed into a student cafeteria, the auditorium into the Arnold and Marie Schwarz Memorial Gymnasium. With undoubtedly the most elegantly furnished arena in the country, the university's basketball team plays its home games before a crowd seated in bleachers built above the former balcony.

Bowling alleys fill the auditorium of the Belmont (1926) in Chicago, the city's last major theater designed by W. W. Ahlschlager.

LOST AND FOUND

With just over 4,000 seats, the Atlantic
City Warner (1929) was just too large for
its boardwalk location.

# TRANSFORMATIONS 3: COMMERCIAL REDEVELOPMENT

Over the past decade a growing number of commercial structures have been adapted for new uses, with everything from train stations to cookie factories converted into shops and restaurants. The movie palaces making this shift are among the most astonishing conversions, as their natural glamor and exotic character heighten an already strong awareness that adapted structures are no longer serving the function for which they were intended.

Some theaters were converted as far back as the Depression, spending years as casino ballrooms, home to the big bands. *Architectural Forum* reported in 1936 that "... the transformation of old theaters into night clubs began as an attempt to turn dark houses into profitable properties." The article had been written to announce the redecoration of the Loew's Ohio in Cleveland, reopening as the Mayfair Casino. The side boxes were replaced by twin curving

staircases, ascending to the balcony from the dance floor (stage). A streamlined bar seating ninety-seven people bisected the grand lobby. Ten years later the Ohio was once again a theater. (The Lamb-designed French Casino of

The Hollywood Playhouse opened in 1927 as a high-class theater. Work was underway in 1980 to turn it into a disco.

The female statues cover themselves modestly while a headless mannequin shows off some merchandise inside the former Southtown Theater (1931) in Chicago.

1938 in Miami Beach reversed the process, going from ballroom to theater.)

The legacy of the ballroom conversions of the Astaire-Rogers era is to be found in more recent days in two theaters that have been turned into discos. In 1978 the Lamar, an art moderne movie house in Jackson, Mississippi, had a dance floor and special lighting installed, courtesy of the Lamar Entertainment Emporium. The legit Hollywood Playhouse (1927) served a number of years as an ABC television

studio before plans were set in 1980 to re-create the interior as the Palace Disco.

In Cleveland, at the border of the rejuvenated Playhouse Square, history chose to repeat itself. Just one door away from the once-converted Ohio Theater, a bar cuts through the lobby of the former Allen Theater (1922). Beneath the repainted lobby rotunda, a salad bar and a ring of tables have been set up.

Storefront conversions began with

the Southtown (1931) in Chicago. This was Rapp & Rapp's last traditional palace and, sadly, one of their least successful. A department store set up cash registers in place of box offices, and replaced the orchestra seating with clothing departments. The Renaissance statuary is permitted to view the scene from a safe distance, not yet called into service as showroom mannequins.

Levy & Klein's Diversey Theater (1924) in Chicago was totally gutted in mid-seventies, a multilevel shopping center taking the place of the auditorium. The Port Theater in Newburyport, Massachusetts, was turned into a furniture showroom. The Magnolia Theater (1948), a late Priteca design, had a sort of floral moderne feel, with more blossoms decorating its surface than any florist shop could contain. In 1975 the Magnolia was converted into a bank.

In Pittsfield, Massachusetts, the Colonial Theatre (1903) was turned into a paint-supply store in 1952. The

The old marquee of the Colonial (1903), *above*, has been put to good use by the new owners of the Pittsfield, Massachusetts theater.

The exotic exterior of the Beverly Theater (1925), in Beverly Hills has been only slightly altered over the years. East Indian styling gave way to art deco, in the thirties; forty years later the stage and seats gave way to a fashionable boutique.

heliport pad installed on the roof has seen infrequent service, but each time it was used the occasion was special. The most celebrated helicopter landing was when Aunt Jemima was flown in to supervise a pancake cookout at the local Lions Club.

Entrepreneurs in two Los Angeles theaters chose to save what remained of the original decor of their palaces. The Beverly (1925), a Beverly Hills theater designed by L. A. Smith, was sold in the seventies to fashion designers, who installed a posh boutique in the former auditorium. The East Indian interior had already been modified in the early 1930s. Elephant statutes at either end of the stage gave way to brightly colored murals. Ultimately this change proved quite appropriate, with the murals serving as backdrop for the stylish mer-

chandise now on display.

The downtown Pantages (1921) after a short stint as a church was turned into the Los Angeles Jewelry Mart. The golden highlights of Priteca's "Pantages Greek" decoration have been retouched and the balcony seats reupholstered, but the character of the Pantages was altered forever when display cases for fur coats were erected in place of the theater's organ screens. A Shower of Light chandelier, left by the church, still hangs above the former auditorium. As a final bizarre touch, old Main Street–style second stories were painted above the jewelry booths at the rear of the former stage. No palace architect, not even John Eberson, ever created such an unusual arrangement.

A temporary art deco remodeling in 1936 converted the Loew's Ohio (1921) in Cleveland into a popular downtown nightclub.

# THE CASE FOR PRESERVATION

The case for preservation has already been made, in part, by the endurance of these eccentric showplaces long past the time of their usefulness. Not all the movie palaces survived, and for most of those that have, changes in appearance and use were inevitable. It would have been pointless to save these buildings solely as heirlooms. Their survival as theaters depended from the start on their capacity to attract customers, their ability to entertain, and their power to dumbfound the beholder. Without such viability, in economic, functional, and visual terms, perhaps the palaces deserve to be relegated to scrapbooks and fond memories.

Fortunately, quite a number of them have proven their worth in the entertainment marketplace. The economic wisdom of reclaiming these structures is now clear, whether for symphony performances, legitimate theater, or religious gatherings. Architecture critics promote such reclamation projects, permitted by a more relaxed architectural climate, to belatedly indulge the palace architects and the ornamental excesses of the golden age.

Now restored or transformed for some strange new career, the majority of the surviving movie palaces are no longer the decaying hulks they were during the 1960s. For those people lucky enough to have seen the palaces before the decline, some of the more extraordinary conversions might appear too drastic and, at times, almost sacrilegious. However, even the most devoted romantic must admit that the *spirit* of the renaissance is welcome, if not always the result. To those for whom this architecture of fantasy is a startling new find, the most bizarre transformation is easily overlooked in favor of just the slightest hint of how it must have felt to witness the theater in its days of glory. A handful of movie houses offer more than just a hint of these feelings. Just as patrons in the early days of motion pictures felt transported by the movies on their screens, the renovated movie palaces carry us back to an earlier age. It is well worth the trip.

# APPENDIX OF THEATERS

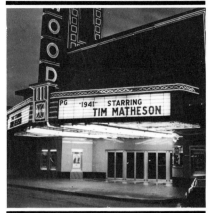

Listed chronologically and alphabetically by theater, (year), location; architect; seating capacity; status as of 1981.

## NINETEENTH CENTURY

Academy of Music (1891), Northhampton, Massachusetts; William Brocklesby; 1,040; movies and performing arts.

Academy of Music (1857), Philadelphia, Pennsylvania; unknown; 2,938; symphony hall.

Auditorium Theatre (1889), Chicago, Illinois; Adler & Sullivan; 4,237; symphony hall.

Goodspeed Opera House (1877), East Haddam, Connecticut; unknown; 200; museum/theater.

Grand Opera House (1871), Wilmington, Delaware; Dixon & Carson; 1,143; performing arts.

Howard Auditorium (Mayfair) (1890), Baltimore, Maryland; unknown; unknown; movies.

Music Hall (1878), Cincinnati, Ohio; Hannaford & Proctor; 3,632; symphony hall.

Pabst Theatre (1895), Milwaukee, Wisconsin; Otto Strack; 1,820; symphony hall.

Port Theatre (unknown), Newburyport, Massachusetts; unknown; unknown; furniture store.

Schiller (Garrick) (1892), Chicago, Illinois; Adler & Sullivan; unknown; razed.

Tainter Memorial (1890), Menomenie, Wisconsin; Ellis; unknown; museum.

## 1900—1905

Colonial Theatre (1903), Pittsfield, Massachusetts; Vance; unknown; paint supply store.

Mahaiwe Theatre (1903), Great Barrington, Massachusetts; unknown; 895; movies.

Majestic (Saxon) (1903), Boston, Massachusetts; John Galen Howard; unknown; movies.

New Amsterdam (1903), New York, New York; Herts & Tallant; 1,100; movies.

## 1906—1910

Academy of Music (1908), Brooklyn, New York; Herts & Tallant; 2,200; symphony hall.

Bijou (1909), Knoxville, Tennessee; unknown; 1,100; performing arts.

Bijou Dream (unknown), Chicago, Illinois; unknown; unknown; razed.

City Photoplays (1910), New York, New York; Thomas W. Lamb; 2,267; razed.

College Theatre (1907), Chicago, Illinois; J. E. O. Pridmore; unknown; razed.

Cort Theatre (1909), Chicago, Illinois; J. E. O. Pridmore; unknown; razed.

Dreamland (1907), Portland, Maine; unknown, unknown; razed.

Hippodrome (1907), Cleveland, Ohio; Knox & Elliot; 4,500; razed.

Majestic (Five Flags) (1910), Dubuque, Iowa; Rapp & Rapp; 717; performing arts.

Metropolitan Opera House (1908), Philadelphia, Pennsylvania; McElfatrick; 3,582; razed.

Moore's (Egyptian) (1907), Seattle, Washington; E. M. Houghton; 2,200; movies and performing arts.

## 1911—1915

Exeter Street Theatre (1914), Boston, Massachusetts; conversion by C. H. Blackall; 900; movies.

Majestic (Paramount) (1915), Austin, Texas; John Eberson; 1,300; performing arts.

Orpheum (1914), Champaign, Illinois; Rapp & Rapp; 800; pornography theater.

Orpheum (American) (1914), St. Louis, Missouri; G. A. Lansburgh; 2,300; legitimate theater.

Orpheum (Capitol) (1913), Salt Lake City, Utah; G. A. Lansburgh; 1,950; performing arts.

Orpheum (Palace) (1911), Los Angeles, California; G. A. Lansburgh; 1,950; movies.

Palace (1914), Manchester, New Hampshire; unknown; 1,000; performing arts.

Pantages (1911), San Francisco, California; B. Marcus Priteca; 1,800; razed.

Pantages (1915), Seattle, Washington; B. Marcus Priteca; 1,418; razed.

Regent (1913), New York, New York; Thomas W. Lamb; 1,845; church.

Ringling Memorial (1915), Baraboo, Wisconsin; Rapp & Rapp; 804; movies.

Spreckel's (1912), San Diego, California; Albright; 1,850; legitimate theater.

Strand (Warner) (1914), New York, New York; Thomas W. Lamb; 2,985; razed.

Wells Theatre (1913), Norfolk, Virginia; unknown; unknown; legitimate theater.

## 1916—1920

Capitol (1919), New York, New York; Thomas W. Lamb; 5,230; razed.

Central Park (1917), Chicago, Illinois; Rapp & Rapp; 1,780; razed.

Coliseum (1916), Seattle, Washington; B. Marcus Priteca; 1,870; movies.

Crandall's Knickerbocker (1917), Washington, D.C.; rebuilt in 1922 by Thomas W. Lamb; 1,457; razed.

Grauman's Million Dollar (1918), Los Angeles, California; W. L. Woollett; 2,345; movies.

Grauman's Rialto (1919), Los Angeles, California; unknown; unknown; razed.

Majestic (Lederer) (1917), Providence, Rhode Island; unknown; 800; multiple legitimate theater.

Mercy (Capitol) (1920), Yakima, Washington; B. Marcus Priteca; 1,800; reconstruction as theater after fire.

Orpheum (1917), New Orleans, Louisiana; G. A. Lansburgh; 2,360; movies.

Palace (1918), Cincinnati, Ohio; Rapp & Rapp; 2,600; closed.

Palace (1918), Washington, D.C.; Thomas W. Lamb; 2,423; razed.

Pantages (1918), Spokane, Washington; B. Marcus Priteca; 1,375; razed.

Pantages (1917), Vancouver, British Columbia; B. Marcus Priteca; 1,600; razed.

Rialto (1916), New York, New York; Thomas W. Lamb; 2,300; razed.

Riviera (1919), Chicago, Illinois; Rapp & Rapp; 1,886; movies.

Rivoli (1917), New York, New York; Thomas W. Lamb; 2,122; movies.

State-Lake (1919), Chicago, Illinois; G. A. Lansburgh; 2,260; movies.

Strand (1918), Dorchester, Massachusetts; unknown; 1,819; performing arts.

Strand (1917), Ithaca, New York; unknown; 1,100; performing arts.

T & D (1916), Oakland, California; Cunningham & Politeo; 2,644; razed.

Victoria (1917), New York, New York; Thomas W. Lamb; 2,394; renovation scheduled for performing arts.

## 1921

Chicago, Chicago, Illinois; Rapp & Rapp; 3,880; movies.

Crown, Pasadena, California; Bennett; 2,200; closed.

Eastman Theater, Rochester, New York; McKim, Mead & White; 3,348; symphony hall.

Golden Gate, San Francisco, California; G. A. Lansburgh; 2,844; legitimate theater.

Loew's Ohio, Cleveland Ohio; Thomas W. Lamb; 1,800; renovation scheduled for performing arts.

Loew's State, Cleveland, Ohio; Thomas W. Lamb; 3,446; renovation in progress for performing arts.

Loew's State, Los Angeles, California; Weeks & Day; 2,450; movies.

Loew's State, New York, New York; Thomas W. Lamb; 3,316; movies.

Majestic, Dallas, Texas; John Eberson; 2,774; performing arts.

Palms-State, Detroit, Michigan; C. Howard Crane; 1,535; movies.

Pantages, Los Angeles, California; B. Marcus Priteca; 1,757; retail jewelry mart.

Roosevelt, Chicago, Illinois; C. Howard Crane; 1,535; razed.

Senate, Chicago, Illinois; W. W. Ahlschlager; 3,097; razed.

Stanley, Philadelphia, Pennsylvania; Thomas W. Lamb; 4,000; razed.

Strand (Michigan), East Lansing, Michigan; John Eberson; 2,000; renovation scheduled for performing arts.

Tivoli, Chattanooga, Tennessee; Rapp & Rapp; 2,300; performing arts.

Tivoli, Chicago, Illinois; Rapp & Rapp; 3,414; razed.

## 1922

Allen, Cleveland, Ohio; C. Howard Crane; 3,009; restaurant and laserium.

Castro, San Francisco, California; Miller & Pflueger; 1,800; revival movies.

Grand Circus (Capitol), Detroit, Michigan; C. Howard Crane; 3,367; closed.

Grauman's Egyptian, Hollywood, California; Meyer & Holler; 1,800; movies.

Loew's State, Boston, Massachusetts; Thomas W. Lamb; 4,000; razed.

Palace, Cleveland, Ohio; Rapp & Rapp; 3,680; performing arts.

Poli Palace, Waterbury, Connecticut; Thomas W. Lamb; 3,419; performing arts.

Warfield, San Francisco, California; G. A. Lansburgh; 2,656; performing arts.

World (Omaha), Omaha, Nebraska; C. Howard Crane; 2,100; closed.

## 1923

Fox, Philadelphia, Pennsylvania; Thomas W. Lamb; 2,457; razed.

Grauman's Metropolitan (Paramount), Los Angeles, California; W. L. Woollett; unknown; razed.

Majestic, Houston, Texas; John Eberson; 2,116; razed.

## 1924

Diversey (Century), Chicago, Illinois; Levy & Klein; 2,966; multilevel shopping center.

Earle (Warner), Washington, D.C.; C. Howard Crane; 2,240; legitimate theater.

Forum, Los Angeles, California; Borgmeyer; 1,800; razed.

Granada, Santa Barbara, California; Rosenthal; 1,800; movies.

Loew's State, St. Louis, Missouri; Thomas W. Lamb; 3,340; men's clothing store.

Pantages, San Diego, California; B. Marcus Priteca; 2,000; razed.

Peery's Egyptian, Ogden, Utah; Hodgson & McClenahan; 1,500; movies.

## 1925

Albee, Brooklyn, New York; Thomas W. Lamb; 3,246; razed.

Alhambra, San Francisco, California; Miller & Pflueger; 1,800; movies, twin.

Beverly, Beverly Hills, California; L. A. Smith; 1,270; boutique and cafe.

Capitol, Chicago, Illinois; John Eberson; 2,416; closed.

Columbia, Longview, Washington; unknown; 1,200; razed.

Embassy, New York, New York; Thomas W. Lamb; 598; movies.

Grand Riviera, Detroit, Michigan; John Eberson; 2,700; closed.

Metropolitan (Music Hall), Boston, Massachusetts; C. H. Blackall; 4,200; performing arts.

Strand, Shreveport, Louisiana; Weil; 2,250; renovation scheduled for performing arts.

Uptown, Chicago, Illinois; Rapp & Rapp; 4,325; movies.

Zaring, Indianapolis, Indiana; Frank Hall; unknown; razed.

## 1926

Academy of Music, New York, New York; Thomas W. Lamb; 2,600; rock shows.

Aladdin, Denver, Colorado; unknown; 908; movies.

Aztec, San Antonio, Texas; R. B. Kelley, with Meyer & Holler; 3,000; movies, triple.

Belasco, Los Angeles, California; Morgan, Walls & Clements; 1,061; church.

Belmont, Chicago, Illinois; W. W. Ahlschlager; 3,257; bowling alleys, closed.

Broadway, Portland, Oregon; Doyle; 1,900 movies, triple.

Carthay Circle, Los Angeles, California; Dwight Gibbs; 1,510; razed.

Congress, Chicago, Illinois; Friedstein, 2,904; movies.

El Capitan (Paramount), Hollywood, California; G. A. Lansburgh; 1,550; movies.

Elsinore, Salem, Oregon; Halford, Bean & Allyn; 1,400; movies.

Fifth Avenue, Seattle Washington; R. C. Reamer; 2,439; legitimate theater.

Granada, Chicago, Illinois; Levy & Klein; 3,448; closed.

Grand Lake, Oakland, California; Reid & Reid; 1,800; movies.

Hollywood, Portland, Oregon; Bennes & Herzog; 1,500; closed.

Loew's State, New Orleans, Louisiana; Thomas W. Lamb; 3,285; movies, triple.

Michigan, Detroit, Michigan; Rapp & Rapp; 4,038; three-level parking garage.

Norshore, Chicago, Illinois; Rapp & Rapp; 2,999; razed.

Olympia (Gusman Center), Miami, Florida; John Eberson; 2,141; performing arts.

Oriental, Chicago, Illinois; Rapp & Rapp; 3,217; closed.

Orpheum, Los Angeles, California; G. A. Lansburgh; 2,350; movies.

Palace, Canton, Ohio; John Eberson; 2,000; renovation scheduled for performing arts.

Palace, Chicago, Illinois; Rapp & Rapp; 2,500; banquet hall and meeting room.

Palace, Columbus, Ohio; Thomas W. Lamb; 3,017; renovation scheduled for performing arts.

Pantages (Orpheum), San Francisco, California; B. Marcus Priteca; 2,500; legitimate theater.

Paramount, New York; Rapp & Rapp; 3,664; razed.

Poli Palace, Worcester, Massachusetts; Thomas W. Lamb; unknown; performing arts.

Proctor's, Schenectady, New York; Thomas W. Lamb; 2,600; performing arts.

Rialto Square, Joliet, Illinois; Rapp & Rapp; 2,800; renovation scheduled for performing arts.

St. Louis (Powell Hall), St. Louis, Missouri; Rapp & Rapp; 3,861; symphony hall.

Shea's Buffalo, Buffalo, New York; Rapp & Rapp; 3,485; performing arts.

Tampa, Tampa, Florida; John Eberson; 1,500; performing arts.

Texas, San Antonio, Texas; Boller Brothers; 2,700; closed.

Valencia, Baltimore, Maryland; John Eberson, 1,400; razed.

## 1927

Alabama, Birmingham, Alabama; Mayger & Graven; 3,000; movies.

Albee, Cincinnati, Ohio; Thomas W. Lamb; 3,292; razed.

Alhambra, Sacramento, California; Starks & Flanders; 1,974; razed.

Avalon, Chicago, Illinois; John Eberson; 2,400; church.

Capitol, Washington, D.C.; Rapp & Rapp; 3,433; razed.

Carolina, Greensboro, North Carolina; Workman & De Sibour; 2,100; performing arts.

Coronado, Rockford, Illinois; F. J. Klein; 2,930; movies.

Egyptian (Ada), Boise, Idaho; Tourtellotte & Hummel; 1,200; movies.

Fox (California), San Jose, California; Weeks & Day; 2,150; closed.

Fox, Stockton, California; Balch & Stanbury; 2,155; closed.

Grauman's Chinese, Hollywood, California; Meyer & Holler; 2,258; movies.

Hollywood, Detroit, Michigan; Mayger & Graven; 3,800; razed.

Hollywood Playhouse, Hollywood, California; Fogerty & Weil; unknown; renovation scheduled as disco.

Indiana, Indianapolis, Indiana; Rubush & Hunter; 3,133; playhouse complex.

KiMo, Albuquerque, New Mexico; Boller Brothers; 1,300; performing arts.

Lerner (Elco), Elkhart, Indiana; K. M. Vitzhum; 2,000; movies.

Loew's Canal, New York, New York; Thomas W. Lamb; 2,379; closed.

Loew's Midland, Kansas City, Missouri; Thomas W. Lamb; 3,800; movies.

Loew's Penn (Heinz Hall), Pittsburgh, Pennsylvania; Rapp & Rapp; 3,486; symphony hall.

Marbro, Chicago, Illinois; Levy & Klein; 3,978; razed.

Mayan, Los Angeles, California; Morgan, Walls & Clements; 1,491; pornography movies.

Missouri, St. Joseph, Missouri; Boller Brothers; 1,391; performing arts.

Oriental, Portland, Oregon; Thomas & Mercier; 2,100; razed.

Orpheum, Omaha, Nebraska; Rapp & Rapp; 2,978; symphony hall.

Orpheum, Seattle, Washington; B. Marcus Priteca; 3,000; razed.

Orpheum, Vancouver, British Columbia; B. Marcus Priteca; 2,874; symphony hall.

Paramount, Abilene, Texas; W. Scott Dunne; 1,407; country music.

Paramount, Palm Beach, Florida; Joseph Urban; 1,000; renovation scheduled for performing arts.

Picadilly, Chicago, Illinois; Rapp & Rapp; 2,500; razed.

Proctor's 86th Street, New York, New York; Thomas W. Lamb; 3,131; razed.

Riviera (Astro), Omaha, Nebraska; John Eberson; 2,800; movies.

Roxy, New York, New York; W. W. Ahlschlager; 5,920; razed.

Saenger, New Orleans, Louisiana; Emile Weil; 3,600; performing arts.

Sheridan, Chicago, Illinois; J. E. O. Pridmore; 2,654; closed.

Stanley, Baltimore, Maryland; Hoffman & Henon; 3,287; razed.

Stanley, Newark, New Jersey; Grad; 1,777; Italian community center.

State, Kalamazoo, Michigan; John Eberson; 1,800; movies.

Tower, Los Angeles, California; S. Charles Lee; 906; movies.

United Artists, Los Angeles, California; C. Howard Crane; 2,214; movies.

# 1928

Ambassador, St. Louis, Missouri; Rapp & Rapp; 3,000; renovation scheduled as dinner theater.

Byrd, Richmond, Virginia; Fred Bishop; 1,384; performing arts.

Capitol (Civic Center), Madison, Wisconsin; Rapp & Rapp; 2,100; performing arts complex.

Capitol (Paramount), Cedar Rapids, Iowa; Peacock & Frank; 1,945; performing arts.

Fabian, Patterson, New Jersey; Wentworth; 3,036; razed.

Fisher, Detroit, Michigan; Mayger & Graven; 2,975; performing arts.

Fox, Brooklyn, New York; C. Howard Crane; 4,088; razed.

Fox, Detroit, Michigan; C. Howard Crane; 5,048; movies.

Fox, Oakland, California; Weeks & Day; 3,300; closed.

Fox, Redondo Beach, California; J. P. Perrine; 1,324; razed.

Keith's, Flushing, New York; Thomas W. Lamb; 2,974; movies, triple.

Keith's Huntington, West Virginia; Thomas W. Lamb; 2,600; movies, triple.

Keith's Memorial (Savoy), Boston, Massachusetts; Thomas W. Lamb; 2,900; opera house.

Kenmore, Brooklyn, New York; Thomas W. Lamb; 3,016; movies.

Loew's Ohio, Columbus, Ohio; Thomas W. Lamb; 2,897; performing arts.

Loew's Richmond, Richmond, Virginia; John Eberson; 2,100; closed.

Loew's State (Landmark), Syracuse, New York; Thomas W. Lamb; 2,908; performing arts.

Loew's State (Ocean State), Providence, Rhode Island; Rapp & Rapp; 3,000; performing arts.

Loew's United Artists, Louisville, Kentucky; John Eberson; 3,273, renovation scheduled as dinner theater.

Minnesota, Minneapolis, Minnesota; Mayger & Graven; 4,050; razed.

Oriental, Milwaukee, Wisconsin; Dick & Bauer; 2,230; revival movies.

Orpheum, Memphis, Tennessee; Rapp & Rapp; 2,400; performing arts.

Palace, Lorain, Ohio; unknown; 1,750; performing arts.

Palace, Marion, Ohio; John Eberson; unknown; performing arts.

Pantages, Fresno, California; B. Marcus Priteca; 2,000; performing arts.

Paradise, Chicago, Illinois; John Eberson, 3,612; razed.

Paramount, Brooklyn, New York; Rapp & Rapp; 4,084; gymnasium.

Paramount, Portland, Oregon; Rapp & Rapp; 3,049; performing arts.

Paramount, Seattle, Washington; Rapp & Rapp; 3,054; performing arts.

Paramount, Toledo, Ohio; Rapp & Rapp; 3,406; razed.

Stanley, Jersey City, New Jersey; Wentworth; 4,332; closed.

Stanley, Pittsburgh, Pennsylvania; Hoffman & Henon; 3,886; performing arts.

Stanley, Utica, New York; Thomas W. Lamb; 2,963; movies and performing arts.

Tennessee, Knoxville, Tennessee; Mayger & Graven; 2,000; closed.

Tower, Philadelphia, Pennsylvania; Hogens & Hill; 3,119; rock shows.

Tulare, Tulare, California; Miller & Pflueger; 1,700; movies.

United Artists, Chicago, Illinois; remodeled by C. Howard Crane; 1,750; movies.

United Artists, Detroit, Michigan; C. Howard Crane; 2,070; gutted.

Uptown, Kansas City, Missouri; John Eberson; 1,600; dinner theater.

Venetian, Racine, Wisconsin; J. E. O. Pridmore; 1,800; razed.

Vita-Temple, Toledo, Ohio; unknown; destroyed by fire in 1933.

## 1929

Avalon, Catalina Island, California; Weber & Spaulding 1,184; movies.

Beacon, New York, New York; W. W. Ahlschlager; 2,657; performing arts.

Fox, Atlanta, Georgia; Mayre, Alger & Vinour; 3,934; performing arts.

Fox, Riverside, California; Balch & Stanbury with L. A. Smith; 1,900; movies.

Fox, St. Louis, Missouri; C. Howard Crane; 5,042; closed.

Fox, San Diego, California; Weeks & Day; 2,876; legitimate theater.

Fox, San Francisco, California; Thomas W. Lamb; 4,651; razed.

Fox (Music Hall), Seattle, Washington; Sherwood Ford; 2,200; nightclub.

Garden, Greenfield, Massachusetts; Wilson; 1,700; movies.

Loew's Akron, Akron, Ohio; John Eberson; 2,987; performing arts.

Loew's Jersey, Jersey City, New Jersey; Rapp & Rapp; 3,300; movies, triple.

Loew's Kings, Brooklyn, New York; Rapp & Rapp; 3,676; closed.

Loew's Paradise, Bronx, New York; John Eberson; 3,884; movies, quadruple.

Loew's Pitkin, Brooklyn, New York; Thomas W. Lamb; 2,817; closed.

Loew's Valencia, Queens, New York; John Eberson, 3,554; church.

Majestic, San Antonio, Texas; John Eberson; 3,700; closed.

Mastbaum, Philadelphia, Pennsylvania; Hoffman & Henon; 4,717; razed.

Paramount, Springfield, Massachusetts; Carlson; 2,147; revival movies.

Patio, Chicago, Illinois; T. H. Buell; 1,500; movies.

Plaza, Kansas City, Missouri; Boller Brothers; 1,950; movies, twin.

Ritz, Corpus Christie, Texas; W. Scott Dunne; 1,500; performing arts.

St. George, Staten Island, New York; De Rosa; 2,956; closed.

Warner (Centre), Milwaukee, Wisconsin; Rapp & Rapp; 2,500; movies, twin.

Warner (Warren), Atlantic City, New Jersey; Hoffman & Henon; 4,185; razed.

## 1930

Fox, Phoenix, Arizona; S. Charles Lee; 1,795; razed.

Fox, Visalia, California; Balch & Stanbury; 1,200; closed.

Fox-Wilshire, Los Angeles, California; S. Charles Lee; 2,500; renovation scheduled for performing arts.

Gateway, Chicago, Illinois; Rapp & Rapp; 2,093; movies.

Hollywood (Mark Hellinger), New York, New York; Thomas W. Lamb; 1,553; legitimate theater.

Loew's 175th Street, New York, New York; Thomas W. Lamb; 3,564; church.

Mayan, Denver, Colorado; unknown; 966; rock shows.

Mayfair (Embassy 2, 3, 4), New York, New York; Thomas W. Lamb; 1,735; movies, triple.

Oriental, Mattapan Square, Massachusetts; Krokyn, Browne & Rosenstein; 2,100; razed.

Pantages, Hollywood, California; B. Marcus Priteca; 2,812; legitimate theater.

Paramount, Denver, Colorado; T. H. Buell; 2,400; performing arts.

Paramount, Fort Wayne, Indiana; Strauss; 2,086; closed.

Pickwick, Park Ridge, Illinois; Harold Zook; 1,200; closed.

Plaza, El Paso, Texas; unknown; 2,000; movies.

Warner, West Chester, Pennsylvania; Rapp & Rapp; 1,626; movies.

## 1931

Fox, Pomona, California; Balch & Stanbury; 1,738; movies.

Fox, Spokane, Washington; R. C. Reamer; 2,350; movies, twin.

Fox-Arlington, Santa Barbara, California; Plunkett & Edwards; 1,825; performing arts.

Fox-Stadium, Los Angeles, California; Boller Brothers; 1,931; closed.

Holland, Bellefontaine, Ohio; Peter Hulsken; 1,400; movies, quintuple.

Los Angeles, Los Angeles, California; S. Charles Lee; 2,190; movies.

Nortown, Chicago, Illinois; J. E. O. Pridmore; 2,086; movies.

Palace, Albany, New York; John Eberson; 3,660; renovation scheduled for performing arts.

Paramount, Aurora, Illinois; Rapp & Rapp; 1,895; performing arts.

Paramount, Oakland, California; Miller & Pflueger; 3,408; performing arts.

Southtown, Chicago, Illinois; Rapp & Rapp; 3,202; department store.

Triboro, Astoria, New York; Thomas W. Lamb; 3,290; razed.

Warner, Erie, Pennsylvania; Rapp & Rapp; 2,585; performing arts.

Warner, Torrington, Connecticut; Thomas W. Lamb; 2,000; movies.

Warner (Power Hall), Youngstown, Ohio; Rapp & Rapp; 2,431; symphony hall.

Warner Brothers, Beverly Hills, California; B. Marcus Priteca; 2,000; closed.

Western (Wiltern), Los Angeles, California; G. A. Lansburgh; 2,334; closed.

## 1932

Fox, Florence, California; S. Charles Lee; 1,800; razed.

Fox, Hackensack, New Jersey; Thomas W. Lamb; 2,230; closed.

Leimert, Los Angeles, California; Morgan, Walls & Clements; 740; church.

Loew's Grand, Atlanta, Georgia; remodeled Thomas W. Lamb; 2,500; razed.

Loew's 72nd Street, New York, New York; Thomas W. Lamb; 3,200; razed.

Paramount, Amarillo, Texas; W. Scott Dunne; unknown; razed.

Paramount, Boston, Massachusetts; A. W. Bowditch; 1,700; renovation scheduled for sound and TV studios.

Radio City Music Hall, New York, New York; Donald Deskey and Rockefeller Center Group; 5,960; movies and stage show.

# 1933—1948

Academy (unknown), Inglewood, California; S. Charles Lee; unknown; church.

Alameda (1933), Alameda, California; Miller & Pflueger; unknown; roller rink.

Alameda (1948), San Antonio, Texas; N. Straus Nayfach; 2,500; movies.

Belmont Shores (unknown), Long Beach, California; unknown; unknown; racquetball courts.

Bruin (unknown), Los Angeles, California; S. Charles Lee; unknown; movies.

Centre (unknown), Denver, Colorado; unknown; 1,275; movies.

Cinema (1938), Miami Beach, Florida; Thomas W. Lamb; unknown; renovation scheduled as shops.

Columbia (unknown), St. Louis, Missouri; unknown; unknown; racquetball courts.

Crest (unknown), Sacramento, California; unknown; unknown; movies.

Esquire (1937), Chicago, Illinois; Pereira & Pereira; 1,390; movies.

Esquire (unknown), Dallas, Texas; unknown; unknown; movies.

Fourth Avenue (unknown), Anchorage, Alaska; B. Marcus Priteca; unknown; movies.

Fox-Westwood Village (unknown), Los Angeles, California; S. Charles Lee; unknown; movies.

Harbor (unknown), Brooklyn, New York; unknown; unknown; racquetball courts.

Hawaii (unknown), Honolulu, Hawaii; C. G. Moeller; 1,100; closed.

Inwood (1941), Dallas, Texas; unknown; unknown; movies.

Lamar (unknown), Jackson, Mississippi; unknown; unknown; disco.

Loyola (unknown), Inglewood, California; S. Charles Lee; unknown; church.

Magnolia (1948), Seattle, Washington; B. Marcus Priteca; 960; bank.

Pekin (unknown), Pekin, Illinois; Elmer F. Behons; unknown, closed.

Penn (1935), Washington, D.C.; John Eberson; 1,438; movies.

Waikiki (1936), Honolulu, Hawaii; C. W. Dickey; 1,300; movies.

Washoe (1936), Anaconda, Montana; B. Marcus Priteca; 1,000; movies.

# BIBLIOGRAPHY

## BOOKS

Dynes, Walter. *Palaces of Europe*. Feltham, Great Britain: Hamlyn Publishing Group, Ltd., 1968.

Francisco, Charles. *The Radio City Music Hall: An Affectionate History of the World's Greatest Theater*. New York: E. P. Dutton, 1979.

Hall, Ben M. *The Best Remaining Seats*. New York: Clarkson Potter, 1961.

Hamlin, Talbot. *Architecture Through the Ages*. New York: Putnam, 1940.

Headley, Robert K., Jr. *Exit: A History of Movies in Baltimore*. Baltimore: published by the author, 1974.

Izenour, George C. *Theatre Design*. New York: McGraw-Hill, 1979.

Krinsky, Carol. *Rockefeller Center*. New York: Oxford University Press, 1978.

Mackay, Constance D'Arcy. *The Little Theater in the United States*. New York: Holt & Co., 1935.

Morrison, Hugh. *Louis Sullivan, Prophet of Modern Architecture*. New York: W. W. Norton & Co., 1935.

*The Ohio Theater*. Columbus: published by the theater, 1978.

Perlman, Daniel H. *The Auditorium Building*. Chicago: Roosevelt University, 1974.

Pildas, Ave, and Lucinda Smith. *Movie Palaces: Survivors of an Elegant Era*. New York: Clarkson Potter, 1980.

Shand, P. Morton. *Motion Picture Houses and Theatres*. Philadelphia: J. B. Lippincott Co., 1930.

Sharp, Dennis. *The Picture Palace*. New York: Frederick A. Praeger, 1969.

Worthington, Clifford. *The Influence of the Cinema on Contemporary Auditorium Design*. London: Pitman & Sons, Ltd., 1932.

## PERIODICALS AND PAMPHLETS

*Marquee*, quarterly journal of the Theatre Historical Society. Notre Dame, Indiana. 1969–.

*Motion Picture News*. 1925–1930.

# INDEX

Page numbers in **bold italic** indicate illustrations.

INDEX

# Society of Architectural Historians Southern California Chapter

# Review

*Wiltern Theatre upper lobby, Photo: Bruce Boehner.*

# THE FUNCTIONS OF DECORATION IN THE AMERICAN MOVIE PALACE

by Karen Safer Polich

During the twentieth century "Eclecticism" was carried to its extreme in the American movie palace where the gamut of historic styles and decorative motifs was adopted profusely and exploited. In major cities across America dozens of movie palaces were erected, displaying a variety of decorative schemes.

In Los Angeles, for example, there was the Million Dollar Theatre, based on Renaissance and Baroque motifs, the Metropolitan Theatre, inspired by ancient, Classical, and Hispano-Persian elements; the Egyptian Theater, copied after an ancient Thebian Temple; the Chinese Theater, executed in emulation of a Cathay Palace; the United Artists' Theater, modeled after Spanish Gothic Cathedrals; the Warner Brothers' Theater in Hollywood, inspired by Romanesque and Moorish examples; the Los Angeles Theater, articulated in the fashion of Louis Quatorze; the Pantages and Wiltern Theaters, decorated in the "moderne" style which was a "geometrication" of ancient and classical motifs.

Such variety was not calculated: theater owners surveyed the community to see what style had not yet been represented and then chose a decorative scheme that was entirely different "so as to make it distinct."[1] Hence, a primary function of the decoration was to distinguish a theater from its neighbor.

In 1927, British historian L' Estrange Fawcett, however, noted that although American movie palaces sometimes maintained a fairly consistent motif, "Louis Quinze or Oriental," more often the decoration was "ludicrously bizarre, a weird medley of all kinds -- Spanish, Indian, Chinese, Egyptian, Gothic, Ojibway, and late Bronx."[2] It was this combining of different decorative motifs that added to the uniqueness of each theater. And it was uniqueness that both theater owner and theatre architect desired, the motivating factor being competition.

Following the First World War, the people of the United States found themselves in the "whirl of a gigantic business boom" where "more wealth was in circulation than anyone had ever dreamed could exist, and . . . more widely distributed than ever before."[3] A new wave of optimism and prosperity pervaded the nation, and as the "necessities of the entire globe concentrated for awhile on the United States," industrial production doubled and purchasing power rose by nearly a fifth.[4]

In the twenties, having for the first time become "urban-centered," America witnessed the growth of a consumer-oriented society shaped in large part by the acceptance of installment buying. As the public was presented with more and more products, businessmen soon realized the immense importance of catering to the desires of the consumer. Studies were conducted by assertive salesmen and advertisers to see what the newly enriched masses wanted (for example, to be young, desirable, rich, in fashion, and envied). Like any other commercial venture, the film industry understood that it was a business; that its ultimate goal was profit. The great showman S.L. Rothafel ("Roxy") acknowledged this fact when, in referring to his theaters, he stated: "It's only business, after all. The idea of doing better than the other fellow is the secret of all success."[5]

Like the salesmen and advertisers, theater owners had to compete for an audience. Bigger budgets and profits in the twenties incited them to compete intensively in building elaborate and luxurious showplaces to attract a public that had more money and time to spend on entertainment (theaters provided recreation and release at a time when people were moving into cities; new labor-saving devices were available at mass-produced prices).

As the competition increased, the architectural forms used by the theater owners became more exaggerated; theater historian Ben M. Hall claimed that the "keener the competition...the more marble the halls became."[6] The "Million Dollar Theater Era" (early 1920's), was one of "unparalleled flamboyance" where there was money to spend, products to buy, hours to dream, and time to exploit affluence; and it was the movie palace that stood out as a shrine to these indulgences.

The belief was held that the distinct decorative character and eclectic nature of each theater contributed to its success. This idea was expressed in the twenties by theater architect W.W. Ahlschlager:

*Modern and recent large theatre design has been seemingly based on the theory of outdoing one's neighbor in the use of marbles, ornamental plaster and polychromed pigments -- the trend in interpretation of such houses has been that if a new house outdid a previous house -- it was considered a successful design.[7]*

*Los Angeles Theatre, (1931, S. Charles Lee, architect) Photo: Bruce Boehner.*

It was observed that the palaces, "splendidly designed and magnificently decorated and equipped," drew an enormously profitable patronage, while the less ornamented theaters lost patrons.[8] The conviction that profuse decoration ensured the success of a theater was a belief generally held by most theater owners. "Bigger and better" was the recipe for success, which was measurable in terms of box-office receipts. L'Estrange Fawcett observed that only twelve films in three years had been responsible for the financial prosperity of the Egyptian Theater (Hollywood), indicating that audiences might have been drawn by something other than the film. Ben Hall supported this idea by stating that it did not really matter what the picture on the screen was; it was secondary to the "total adventure."

It was, however, the film producers who most realized the appeal of the movie palace as they vied for exhibition of their films at premiere houses like Grauman's Chinese or Egyptian, where commercial success was almost guaranteed due to the attraction of the theater itself. Hence, a major function of decoration was to attract the public by impressive decorative schemes to ensure the success of the film product -- which additionally mean ensuring the success of the film theater.

Regardless of the particular decorative schemas manifest by any single movie palace, the overriding impression of opulence was what attracted the audience. The visual impact of prodigious and meticulously realized detail was registered first and foremost;

*Texaco Building/United Artists Theatre (1927, Walker & Eisen, architects; C. Howard Craine, interiors) Photo: Bruce Boehner.*

style was secondary. Numerous magazine and newspaper articles appearing in the twenties included detailed accounts of the theaters which help to convey a sense of the overwhelming impact that ornament had on the patron. For example, an article in <u>Los Angeles Saturday Night</u>, which reviewed the Gala Dedicatory Premiere of the United Artists' Theater (1927), also described the exterior and interior of the theater building:

*The effect of old stone-work is splendidly achieved on the walls themselves. Panels of mellowed stone, treated in dull polychrome, picked out with old gold and grayed-off primary colors, and the intricately carved half-corbels and the tracery screens over the huge procenium arch and the side walls, all give an indescribable air of an ancient Castilian edifice. The two great lobbies are, likewise, masterpieces of decoration, with solid arched ceilings, carved in elaborate designs. The intermediate lobby gives the*

*effect of old cathedral glass windows, with their soft, mellow richness relieved by touches of gold embroidery on the costumes of the painted figures. The corridors and stairways reflect the same general scheme, and the entire ceiling of the main lobby is handled to give the appearance of an old medieval tapestry.[9]*

This, and hundreds of other descriptions of the theaters, indicated the atmosphere of "conspicuous consumption" that was created for the moviegoer. As Lucinda Smith has suggested, there was "too much to see in only one visit" -- precisely the hope of the theater owner.[10] Indeed, Smith's assumption that the

*Detail, Texaco Building/United Artists Theatre, (1927, Walker & Eisen, architects; C. Howard Craine, interiors) Photo: Bruce Boehner.*

"movie palace was easily the most splendid structure most patrons had ever seen," is quite plausible.

That the public was awed by the sumptuous decoration was understandable, but what is most interesting is why the public was attracted. It has been suggested that after the First World War there was a ubiquitous "curiosity about the lives of the rich and their surroundings."[11] In part, Hollywood satisfied this curiousity by presenting films in the twenties that featured the "smart middle class heroes and heroines moving in a world of motorcars, steamships and elegant homes...the backgrounds had to conform to a popular, Hollywood inspired concept of affluence."[12] And Craig Morrison has suggested that

*. . . There was a small class of people living in the sort of luxury portrayed on film. Many of those people were newly moneyed*

*Theatre interior, Warner Brothers Western Theatre (now Wiltern Theatre)/Pellissier Building (1930-31, Morgan, Walls & Clements, architects with G. A. Lansburgh and Anthony B. Heinsbergen) Photo: Bruce Boehner.*

*industrialists or inventors, and the tired shop girl who sat on a throne in the lobby of Lowe's Akron probably owned a few shares of stock and dreamed of a day when she could realistically expect to live permanently in the sort of splendor to which her admission ticket had temporarily admitted her.* [13]

Indeed, as Morrison implied, the cinema of the twenties was to a large extent directed toward a female audience. Producers based their decisions of what the public wanted on the assumption that "movies must appeal to and excite, but not harm, the women of America." [14] Feminine taste and its promotion was being cultivated by mass-circulation magazines such as Ladies Home Journal and House Beautiful; however, taste was being shaped primarily by the cinema. According to Russell Lynes, the art directors of films established themselves as "purveyors of taste on a scale which even editors of mass-circulation magazines could not attain. [15] Sets were built for the films with intricate ornamental detail and furnished in opulent period decor that made housewives' mouths water.

Inevitably, in an age of mass consumption, the movies influenced the tastes and aspirations of the masses. Movies presented standards of dress, furnishings, and social behavior hithertofore unknown to millions who had never seen the inside of elegant

hotels, restaurants or private villas. Where luxury hotels, opera houses, and other structures built and used by the socially elite were closed to the public, movie palaces provided an accessible and classless entertainment form. Hailed as "shrines of democracy where no patron was privileged over another," the movie palaces afforded a standard of comfort and opulence unknown in the everyday lives of the public. The suggestion has been made that for millions the cinema became a dream world in which they could indulge their fantasies of wealth and escape from the monotony of life, which was increasingly being standardized by mass production.

In an attempt to reflect the tastes of the public and so attract their attention and patronage, theater architects adopted styles they believed the public wanted. Thomas Lamb stated that his allegiance to the Adam Brothers' style was based on the grounds that it reflected the "mood and preference of the American people." As an observer of the people's tastes, Lamb accordingly changed his choice of styles in 1925 when he wrote that he:

*. . . noted a lessening in response of the average patron to the charm of architectural backgrounds patterned after the works of the Adam Brothers. There was an underlying demand for something more gay, more flashy -- a development for which there*

*Detail, Mayan Theatre (1927, Morgan, Walls & Clements, architects) Photo: Bruce Boehner.*

*is much precedent in the history of architecture. For this reason, I began to favor in my design an entirely different style, leaning toward the periods of Louis XVI and the very rich productions of the Italian Baroque style.* [16]

While sufficient documentation cannot be found to definitely support the fact that these theaters actually reflected the taste of the public, the statement can be made that the theaters were popular, as evidenced by the high attendance, as can also be suggested that the movie palaces reflected the tastes of the theater owners and architects who thought they knew what would please the public (a belief confirmed by box-office receipts). Regardless of what they might or might not reflect, the movie palaces were important art forms. While the structures were not taken seriously by the cultural arbiters of the day, reexamination of their social and economic implications have brought them to the attention of today's architectural historians.

Following in the continuum of the "decorative tradition," the movie palace's decorative scheme functioned to distinguish the individual theater, to impress the viewer with its opulence, and to reflect the desires of the public for richness. Additionally, the function of the decoration was to express the purpose of the building -- that is, entertainment and fantasy. The electric

*California Theatre (1918, A. B. Rosenthal, architect) Photo: Bruce Boehner.*

*Detail, Los Angeles Theatre, (1931, S. Charles Lee, architect)*
*Photo: Bruce Boehner.*

lights, decorative facade, attractive box-office, and patterned terrazzo pavement all functioned as symbols of entertainment that attracted the prospective customer so that he or she would buy an admission ticket. The facade spelled out fun, enchantment, and escape to the masses who needed to "lose themselves" in fantasy.

A most important part of the idea underlying the use of decoration was the desire to make patrons feel like millionaires. The "murals, rock- crystal chandeliers, mahogany paneling" and so on were all part of an affluent image used by promoters to entice customers into the world of richness missing from their homes. It has been suggested that the theater architect was an "escape artist," whose mission was to build "new dream worlds for the disillusioned."[17] And according to S. Charles Lee, the movie palace architect stole his psychology "straight from the church," stating that like the cathedral, the movie palace gave the people what was missing from their daily lives: "religion, solace, art, and most important, a feeling of importance."[18]

As has been shown, decoration functioned to give an illusion of wealth equivalent to the glamour that was being shown on the screen; and, smart exhibitors capitalized on the glamorous climate being created in the movies a shrewdly "cashed in on the public's thirst for wealth and fantasy."[19] In an attempt to appeal to the

aspirations and tastes of the public to generate profits, theater owners "carefully calculated" the effects of ornamentation. They tried to impress the public and spared no expense in so doing. Perhaps theater architect John Eberson stated the rationale behind the decoration most succinctly with his alliterative slogan "Prepare Practical Plans for Pretty Playhouses -- Patrons Pay Profits." Indeed, businessmen realized the potential profit to be gained by elaborately decorating their theaters. And, while aesthetics was probably not their major consideration, a concept of "beauty" was identified as the means by which to attract the public and generate great profits.

The functions of decoration were both traditional and novel. Decoration functioned to indicate that the building was "important"; that is, it indicated the status of the film industry and the theater owner (decoration being equated with wealth). It also reflected the prosperity of a nation temporarily rich from war. Most significantly, however, it made the patron feel important because he or she was provided entertainment in the surroundings of traditionally elitest decoration -- produced in the theaters for the use and enjoyment of the masses.■

*Detail, Metropolitan Water District Building/Million Dollar Theatre (1918, A. C. Martin, architect; William L. Woolett, interiors) Photo: Bruce Boehner.*

NOTES:

1. *The Story of the Films*, p. 265, cited by D. J. Wenden, *The Birth of the Movies* (New York: E.P. Dutton, 1975), p. 123.

2. L' Estrange Fawcett, *Films: Facts and Forecasts* (Pall Mall, England: Geoffrey Bles, 1927), p. 85.

3. Benjamin B. Hampton, *A History of the Movies* (New York: Covici Friede Publishers, 1931), p. 203.

4. Jeffrey L. Meikle, *Twentieth Century Limited* (Philadelphia: Temple University Press, 1979), p. 7.

5. *Green Book* magazine, quoted in Ben M. Hall's *The Best Remaining Seats* (New York: Clarkson N. Potter, Inc., 1961), p. 37.

6. Hall, *The Best Remaining Seats*, p. 17.

7. "The Aim for Beauty and Utility," quoted in Ben M. Hall, *The Best Remaining Seats*, p. 91.

8. Hampton, *A History of the Movies*, p. 305.

9. "Southland's Finest Theater Completed," *Los Angeles Saturday Night* 8 (10 December 1927): 2.

10. Lucinda Smith, *Movie Palaces* (New York: Clarkson N. Potter, Inc. 1980), p. 8.

11. Hall, *The Best Remaining Seats*, p. 17.

12. Wenden, *The Birth of the Movies*, p. 110.

13. Craig Morrison, "From Nickelodeon to Picture Palace and Back," *Design Quarterly*, no. 93 (1974), p. 15.

14. Wenden, *The Birth of the Movies*, p. 114.

15. Russell Lynes, *The Tastemakers* (New York: Harper and Brothers, 1954) pp. 228–229.

16. Thomas Lamb, quoted in Ben M. Hall, *The Best Remaining Seats*, pp. 106, 109.

17. Hall, *The Best Remaining Seats*, p. 94.

18. Interview with S. Charles Lee, S. Charles Lee & Associates, Beverly Hills, California, 28 April 1980.

19. Hall, *The Best Remaining Seats*, p. 17.

# The Planning of Colonial Los Angeles

by Candida Burke

*This paper won SAH/SCC's Second Prize in our chapter's first scholarship competition for students in Southern California. Ms. Burke was awarded $50. Ms. Burke is currently studying Community Design and Planning in the School of Landscape Architecture, College of Environmental Science and Forestry, State University of New York at Syracuse. She has a undergraduate degree in Biology from Sonoma State College. Ms. Burke is a seventh generation Californian, whose ancestry traces back to the period of Spanish colonization of California. Her permanent residence is in the Silverlake district of Los Angeles, barely five miles from El Pueblo -- the colonial center of Los Angeles. Her photos accompany the article.*

The Spaniards explored and colonized the Americas for nearly three hundred years. It became necessary during that time to develop a system of laws and guidelines to ensure that the interests of the Crown were served in the distant lands. This paper will briefly describe the evolution of instructions which led to the creation of 148 City Planning Ordinances which were distributed to explorers and officials responsible for colonization of the New World. Then, as exemplified by Los Angeles, it will show how some of the ordinances were applied in the field and the community form which they produced.

Early instruction left all major decisions concerning settlement to the discretion of the explorer. An example of such instructions are those from King Ferdinand, delivered to Nicolas de Ovando in 1501:

*As it is necessary in the island of Espanola to make settlements, and from here it is not possible to give precise instructions, investigate the possible sites, and in conformity with the quality of the land and sites, as well as with the present population outside present settlements, establish settlements in the numbers and in the places that seem proper to you. [1]*

However, subsequent instructions given to Pedrarias Davila in 1513 contained the foundations of rational city planning [2]. These foundations would continue to be built upon and revised for the next sixty years, culminating in a compilation of the decrees and mandates regarding the founding and building of settlements. The compilation took the form of 148 City Planning Ordinances which were issued in 1573 by King Felipe II. This compilation was one of many areas of legislation governing the New World territories; however, these 148 Ordinances were published separately to expedite their distribution. The first complete text of Spanish legislation for the new territories was not finished until 1681 by the Council of the Indies [3]. The City Planning Ordinances, contained within these Laws of the Indies, in terms of their widespread application and comprehensive instructions are considered among the most remarkable and effective planning documents ever used in history.

The main objectives of the Spanish Empire in the New World were conquest, cultural imperialism, and the conversion of native peoples to Christianity [4]. The City Planning Ordinances were a tool used to achieve these objectives and serve as guidelines for site selection, physical form and political organization of the settlement. In this way, they incorporated familiar elements into an organized plan which could be easily applied to a variety of geological locations by unskilled workers. [5]

An investigation of the early history of the city of Los Angeles reveals that the City Planning Ordinances of the Laws of the Indies were instrumental in the presettlement planning and resultant physical town layout. Before examining the founding of the settlement, it is of interest to review the first thorough exploration of the area by Europeans, for that followed the instructions put forth in the City Planning Ordinances.

January 9, 1769, was the beginning of an effort to start colonization in Alta California by the Spaniards. On this date, the first of three ships and two overland parties set out with Don Gaspar de Portola having been appointed as leader of the expedition and governor of upper California [6]. The group reached San Diego and began construction of a settlement which would be used as a supply base for future ventures. It was

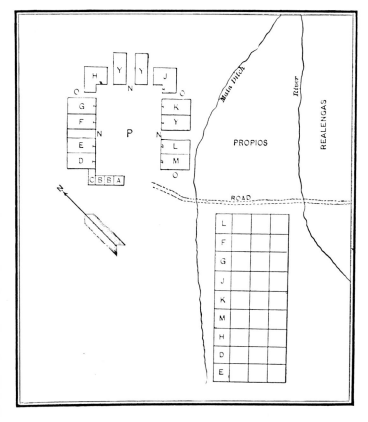

Map of Los Angeles in 1786. In the upper left is the rectangular plaza with its corners oriented to the directions of the compass. With the exception of the southwest side of the plaza, the streets are entering as prescribed by the City Planning Ordinances of the Laws of the Indies. On the right half of the map are agricultural fields. This map is from Bancroft's History of California.

decided that Father Junipero Serra would remain in San Diego while Portola continued the expedition accompanied by four officers, two Fanciscan priests, many soldiers and muleteers. It was on this, the first overland exploration of upper California by Europeans, that we have a written description of the valley which was to become the site of the pueblo, the city, and finally the metropolis of Los Angeles. Documented by Father Juan Crespi, the description of August 2, 1769, reads as follows:

*After traveling about a league and a half through a pass between low hills, we entered a very spacious valley, well grown with cottonwoods and alders, among which ran a beautiful river... this plain where the river ran was very expansive. It had good land for planting all kinds of grain and seeds...it has all the requisites for a large settlement... After crossing the river we entered a large vineyard of wild grapes and an infinity of rose bushes in full bloom. All the soil is black and loamy, and is capable of producing every kind of grain and fruit which may be found. [7]*

After meeting the native Indian population and christening the river "El Rio de Nuestra Senora La Reina de Los Angeles de Porciuncula," (now the Los Angeles river) the explorers continued their trek in a northerly direction.

When comparing these events with instructions from the ordinances, their correlation can be easily followed. The first of the City Planning Ordinances specifies that only those persons with "license and approval" shall make discovery in the new lands. The expedition led by Portola was sent by the Vistador General, Don Jose Galvez, with instructions to secure possession of upper California for the Spanish Crown. Ordinances thirteen and fourteen direct the explorers to "take possession... perform the necessary ceremonies and writs" and to "name each land, each province and the mountains and principal rivers they might encounter." These tasks were performed by Portola and his men throughout the journey; the naming of the Los Angeles river is but one example.

The founding of the pueblo on the Los Angeles river was in response to a royal proclamation of September 10, 1772, which mandated the establishment of presidios along the northern frontier of the Empire [8]. The purpose of these new settlements was to create an agricultural base from which to provide supplies for soldiers and to minimize dependence upon the expanding mission system and shipments from Mexico.

*The site of the original plaza of Los Angeles is no longer exactly known. In 1815, a flood swept away or badly damaged at least half of the pueblo, resulting in the relocation of the plaza to is present-day site. Several alterations have been made to the plaza through the years. The gazebo, added in 1870 is in the foreground of this view taken from within the plaza. In the background are the Pico House built in the 1860's and City Hall.*

Several prerequisites for the selection of sites for settlement are made in the City Planning Ordinances, most notable and detailed are ordinances numbered 34 through 41. These are briefly summarized in Ordinance 111 before further instructions directing the layout of a new settlement are given:

*Having made the selection of the site where the town is to be built, it must, as already stated, be in an elevated and healthful location; be with means of fortification; have fertile soil and with plenty of land for farming and pasturage; have fuel, timber and resources; have fresh water, a native population, ease of transport, access and exit; and be open to the north wind; and, if on the coast, due consideration should be paid to the quality of the harbor and that the sea does not lie to the south or west; and if possible not near lagoons or marshes in which poisonous animals and polluted air and water breed.*

When these instructions are compared with the description by Father Crespi, it is already possible to see how the site of Los Angeles had many of the features which were desired.

Inducements of land, money, supplies and honor were offered to those who would come to be settlers in upper California. Upon arrival each new family was to receive a house lot, two irrigable and two non-irrigable agricultural lots, livestock, tools, a branding iron and a salary for a predetermined length of time. [9] After succeeding to carry out their commitment, the building of a new town, the founding families and their descendants were bestowed with the title and honor of hijosdalgo, or illustrious men of known ancestry. [10]

After the area, province and site have been selected and development opportunities determined for a new settlement the Governor was to decide to what extent it should be populated. [11] Ordinance 89 suggests that at least thirty neighbors are desirable for the establishment of a new settlements. Ordinance 100 states that there should be no less than twelve persons but Ordinance 101 adds that it is possible to start a settlement at a preselected location if there are ten married men who volunteer. In the case of Los Angeles there were eleven families, totaling forty-four persons who were recruited from the regions of Sonora and Sinaloa in Mexico. [12]

*In 1926, a campaign to renovate the then dilapidated original center of Los Angeles was started. The Avila adobe was saved from demolition and in 1930 Olvera Street was closed to traffic and transformed into a Mexican Marketplace. In 1953, 44 acres became the El Pueblo de Los Angeles State Historic Park. This view is taken from Olvera Street looking toward the plaza.*

The size of the plaza was to be determined by the number of expected settlers who would inhabit the pueblo. Maximum, minimum and ideal dimensions for plazas were given and supported by their appropriateness for the celebration of fiestas and accomodation of horse and carriage traffic.[13] Further provisions were made for the creation of secondary plazas in conjunction with religious buildings as the settlements expanded.

Considerable importance was placed upon the central public square of new settlements in the Americas. The public square became the focal point around which the town plan was designed. It was here where formal ceremonies and daily social activities took place, and the residents and visitors developed a sense of the civic identity of the community.[15]

Ordinance 112 states that the main plaza should be the "starting point" of the new settlement, its goes on to specify the preferred location for plazas in coastal and inland sites. In the case of inland sites, the main plaza was to be at the "center of town" and the city was to radiate from there.

The first lot assigned after the plaza and streets were laid out was to be dedicated as the site of the main church.[16] Specific design criteria for buildings surrounding the plaza encouraged a finished product which focused maximum prestige upon the temple. No buildings were to be placed near the temple so that it could be decorated and seen from all directions, and it was preferred that it be raised above ground level so that it must be approached by steps.[17]

Of interest to today's landscape architects, architects and planners is the use of a concept that incorporated the public plaza with adjacent public buildings, those of church and governmental functions. The ordinances say that after the church site has been chosen, sites for the royal council, cabildo house, customs house and arsenal were to be "located in such a manner that in times of need one may aid the other."[18] Therefore, these buildings were located on the perimeter of the plaza. This placement of public buildings, along with the intended public nature of the plaza is further reinforced in Ordinance 126 which says "in the plaza, no lots shall be assigned to private individuals."

As much as possible, climatic factors were considered in the design of plazas and surrounding streets. It was suggested that the orientation of the plaza be arranged so that the streets running off it would not gather and channel wind, therefore making the plaza, as well as the streets, more comfortable.[19] Considerations of temperature were also taken when specifying street width, and covered walkways were an amenity which was greatly encouraged to allow for more comfort during hot, sunny and rainy weather.[20]

Governor de Neve worked out the details of the physical town form in advance of the arrival of settlers from Mexico. He staked out four square leagues to be divided into parcels for agricultural fields, pasture and range lands, private homes and public and church buildings, all surrounding a small plaza. The plaza and street layout depicted in a map of Los Angeles, believed to have been made for de Neve, represents close approximation to the size and form mandated in the City Planning Ordinances. The plaza was dimensioned at 206 feet by 275 feet, smaller than the minimum specified size, yet the general form and orientation were in accordance with specifications in that the plaza was rectangular and the corners pointed to the directions of the compass. The guard house, public granary, government house and chapel were situated on lots surrounding the plaza. There is also evidence found in a drawing made of Los Angeles in 1857 that supports the use of a long colonaded walkway along a main street.

*The large enclosed courtyard of the Avila adobe, the oldest existing house in Los Angeles, was typical of the Spanish Colonial style.*

Many of the concepts contained within the City Planning Ordinances were borrowed from Greek and Roman planning theory.[21] The Roman ideal city consisted of a package of elements which were necessary for its social and political functioning. The Spaniards followed this same vein in their colonial town planning; with the combination of public plaza, church, municipal buildings, private homes and common pasture land, the whole of a functioning and interdependent town was created. Even though Los Angeles was founded on the periphery of the Spanish Empire near the end of its reign, this basic image of a Spanish colonial town came into existence. The historical importance and aesthetic and functional value of the City Planning Ordinances have been recognized in recent years as is demonstrated in efforts made to preserve and enhance the original core of Los Angeles. ∎

To the northwest of the post-flood plaza is the Plaza Catholic Church which was constructed between 1818 and 1820.

NOTES:

1. Dan Stanislawski, "Early Spanish Town Planning in the New World," *The Geographic Review*, Vol. XXXVII, No. 1, (January 1945) p. 95.

2. Ibid.

3. Dora Crouch, *Spanish City Planning in North America*, Cambridge Massachusetts, 1982, p. 26.

4. Dora Crouch, "The City Planning Ordinances of the Laws of the Indies Revisited," *Town Planning Review*, Vol. 48, (October 1948), p. 135.

5. Dora Crouch, *Spanish City Planning in North America*, Cambridge Massachusetts, 1982, p. xvii.

6. David L. Clark, *Los Angeles: A City Apart*, Woodland Hills, California, 1981, p. 11.

7. Ibid., p. 88.

8. Ibid.

9. Dora Crouch, *Spanish City Planning in North America*, Cambridge Massachusetts, 1982, p. 157.

10. Ordinance 99.

11. Ordinance 43.

12. David L. Clark, *Los Angeles: A City Apart*, Woodland Hills, California, 1981, p. 34.

13. Ordinance 112.

14. Ordinance 118.

15. Dora Crouch, *Spanish City Planning in North America*, Cambridge Massachusetts, 1982, p. 42.

16. Ordinance 119.

17. Ordinance 124.

18. Ordinance 121.

19. Ordinance 114.

20. Ordinance 115.

21. Francis Violich, "Evolution of the Spanish City," *American Institute of Planning Journal*, (August 1967), pp. 172, 177.

# A Different View of the Center of Los Angeles

## by Richard Rosen

*This paper won SAH/SCC's First Prize in our chapter's first scholarship competition for students in Southern California. Mr. Rosen was awarded $200. Mr. Rosen is working toward a Master's Degree in Urban Planning. He has a Bachelor of Arts Degree in Architecture from the University of Pennsylvania. He currently resides in Long Beach. Mr. Rosen's photographs accompany the article.*

*"Widely projecting cornices of richly modeled architectural terra cotta..." The Biltmore Hotel (1922–23, Schultze & Weaver, architects)*

In Reyner Banham's book, <u>Los Angeles / The Architecture of Four Ecologies</u>, which examines the social and architectural history of metropolitan Los Angeles, there is one brief chapter which is devoted to downtown Los Angeles. The chapter opens with the title "A Note On Downtown" and the text continues immediately with the words "because that is all downtown Los Angeles deserves." Banham takes the time to discuss downtown not because he sees it as being worthy of examination in its own right, but rather to illustrate a larger theme. This larger theme is a celebration of the mobility, the freedom, the very un-rootedness that make Los Angeles so distinctive and unique and which have, according to Banham, rendered downtown "irrelevant."

These qualities of mobility and rootlessness in Los Angeles have disturbed professional planners and architectural historians for so many decades that this metropolis has come to be widely perceived as the very harbinger of universal urban doom. Banham has little patience with this view. Indeed, one of the basic postures of his book is that of a counterattack against all those who have been so busy vilifying or trying to change Los Angeles that they've been unable to perceive its vitality and unique beauty.

Thus in the chapter on downtown Banham follows his initial remark about the district's pointlessness with the comment that "this opinion will undoubtedly offend entrenched downtown interests and historians who still feel that the development of the city must in some way follow consequentially from the foundation of the pueblo..." And he begins his conclusion of the chapter with a reference to the recent high rise developments which have been "underwritten by... money from the east that will never know how to go with the flow of Angeleno life."

In short, Banham minimizes the importance of downtown as a magnet and as the root of subsequent metropolitan growth, both to reinforce his theme of freedom and mobility, and to defend these characteristics. I, however, can't help but think that Banham's vision is at least in part a reflection of the true Angeleno's attitude towards his city, which consists of a stubborn refusal to accept this settlement as most definitely a city.

*"Elaborate cast iron streetlight standards..." Sixth Street west of Olive*

need not look far to find manifestations of this attitude. ...bers of my extended family have been migrating here for ...erations and many have watched the metamorphosis of the ...ropolitan area from a settlement of single family homes recently ...uted from pastures and orange groves, to a dense, apartment ...commerce filled city, erupting with high-rise buildings. This ...vitable development is universally viewed by my family with ...rmous regret and often with outright hostility. This ...-urban bias also explains why Los Angeles alone among major ...erican cities (with the exception of Washington, D.C.) ...ared a remarkable 150-foot legal limit on the allowable height ...ll buildings -- save city hall -- during a period when the ...ropolitan area was expanding at a rate that left it second most ...ulous urban region in the United States at the time this ...triction was finally lifted in 1957.

...he United States, our collective urban mythology holds that ...prominence of a city's skyline is the quintessential symbol of ...competence and power as a community. The question ...ediately arises: was the skyline of Los Angeles limited due to ...possibility of earthquakes here? Research uncovers no ...ence that the height restriction, in effect since 1905 (a year ...re the great San Francisco quake) was created or maintained ...fear of dangers related to earthquake tremors. Rather the ...ence indicates that the purpose of this limitation was to guide ...city's growth "along broad and harmonious lines of beauty and ...metry." Specifically, the city consciously chose, by a ...-wide popular vote, to impose this height restriction, thereby ...cting a city-image of power and dynamism and consequently ...erating the low profile image which Los Angeles retained for so ...j.

...ther manifestation of a deep Angeleno anti-city bias is the ...rly universal disdain for downtown that one finds out here, an ...tude which certainly does not come from an actual familiarity ...what is to be found in the district. Instead it appears to ...ive from a deeply felt conviction that whatever is there could ...possibly be something with which one would want to identify ...1. And of course, what people see in their environment is ...red by their preconceptions about it. Thus when the average ...geleno does venture downtown, it is no surprise that upon ...val, he or she usually sees only congestion, ugliness, ...rder and blight.

And what of the professional city planners and architectural historians; how have they perceived downtown? Victor Gruen in his book The Heart of Our Cities stated that "the core of Los Angeles... is not only small in size but void of true urban life as well." He went on to claim that "what remain in the heart of that mighty metropolis are the structures serving public administration, the remnants of the original headquarters of banks and corporations (insignificant in comparison with their enormous branches)... and a park, which is a hangout of those unfortunate characters who cannot find their place in society, the bums." Although these remarks were published in 1964, before the explosion of development along the Bunker Hill - Flower Street corridor, it is important to note that they also predate much of the deterioration which has taken place on downtown's east side. In any case, this is what Gruen, a widely respected city planner saw in 1964.

I, myself, am newcomer to Southern California. I arrived here in January of 1982 from Philadelphia, Pennsylvania where I had lived happily in the heart of town for the previous fifteen years. Needless to say, I love city life. Other than that bias, however, any specific preconceptions I may have had about downtown Los Angeles were drawn primarily from the Automobile Club map of the area, which I had studied in detail before I arrived. From this map downtown looked pretty interesting, what with a fairly extensive Chinatown, a "Little Tokyo," the second largest garment district in the United States and on and on and on. Once here I wasted no time in familiarizing myself with the built environment, and much of that time has been spent exploring downtown. What I have found there is an extremely rich, intense, magnetic and exciting place.

*"Colored flags draped from projecting flag poles..."* Union Bank Building on Sixth Street

II

Speeding south on the Hollywood Freeway, a motorist rapidly approaches the skyline of downtown Los Angeles. Decelerating to take in the sharp curve of the ramp on to the Harbor Freeway and then following this curve around, the driver checks back over his left shoulder for merging traffic speeding towards him through the stack, and then quickly blends in with this traffic. He accelerates again and... glancing off to the left: the skyline, which had been an abstract silhouette visible above the freeway landscaping, rapidly recomposes itself and stretches out now into a range of skyscrapers, a densely packed wall of towers, filling the visual space to the left and beginning with the County Health Department Building close by and resting on the foot of Bunker Hill below, this same short hill crowned by the handsome Water and Power Building above, a glimpse of the Dorothy Chandler Pavilion behind.

Guiding his car into the lane marked "110 South/6th St." the driver finds himself rapidly diverging from the through-traffic lanes and as rapidly rising in elevation, until he looks down on the same flow of traffic he had only just merged into. At a higher elevation still are bridges which he passes under – one, two, three – carrying cross traffic overhead, the drivers in the cars on these bridges looking down on him looking down on the river of cars flowing below, all the while concrete ramps plunging down and entering and exiting the freeway below from the bridges above.

At the same time, visible under and over the bridges and ramps, are the individual elements of the range of skyscrapers continuing off to the left; the short, frontal peaks of the Bunker Hill Apartments, in the shadows of the prominently skewed Security Pacific Tower, the smooth surfaced Crocker Center wedges behind, and the tight skinned silver-green profile of the Wells Fargo Bank Tower beyond that. All these swiftly merge and recede as the prismatic Sheraton Grande Hotel comes into focus in the foreground right up at the freeway's edge, just in front of the low bronze glass cylinders of the Bonaventure. The Union Bank Tower steps forward in front of the Bonaventure, the tower defined at its edges by the pattern of sunlight penetrating the gap between its silver-sheathed vertical piers and its recessed enclosing surface. Finally, the stark, cold, black bulk of Arco Center's twin towers emerges from the background at the same time as the towering First Interstate Bank Building, taller than any of the other structures downtown and climaxing the ride.

*"Richly planted rooftop garden..."* Pacific Mutual Building

The driver decelerates again, following the Sixth Street exit ramp around off to the left and, plunging into the heart of the mass of buildings that is downtown, he glides to a dead stop at the red light on Figueroa Street.

The entire experience just described takes approximately ninety seconds and it compares favorably with any of the most famous urban vistas in America. It does so, not because the buildings involved are big; there are several American cities with skylines made up of many much larger structures, and not because the individual buildings involved are distinguished, although several of the recent structures clearly fall into that category. Instead, the experience is exhilarating because of the singular way in which skyline, buildings, freeway and driver interact to generate a dynamic kinetic experience, an experience with sensations of both individual freedom and deeply rooted power; the freedom, justly celebrated by Banham in his book and monumentalized by the freeway; the power, bubbling beneath the surface for decades and erupting into its own monument – the skyline – after the height limitation was lifted in 1957.

III

But even after experiencing and appreciating this particular view of the skyline and even after all the exploring I'd done, I don't believe that I had a clear focus on the center of Los Angeles until I made an excursion to San Diego and began touring the downtown of that sister city to the south. It was the brevity of San Diego's core – in its area, height and density – which first indicated to me the true intensity of downtown Los Angeles.

Before I went to San Diego I witnessed many times another view of downtown Los Angeles - the view one sees as one approaches downtown from the east and passes it to the south on the Santa Monica Freeway. I noticed that this view takes in an extremely large area (basically all of downtown as defined by the freeway loop of which the Santa Monica forms the southern link.) I also noted that the entire area between the distant skyscrapers in this view and the freeway on which I was traveling appeared to be filled with a dense stew of commercial activity and buildings, including an expansive middle ground of ten to thirteen floor structures and a larger foreground of lower buildings. But the immense scale of this district only became apparent to me in contrast with the intimacy of downtown San Diego, whose entire extent could fit into Los Angeles' central freeway loop five times over. What's more, this freeway loop by no means describes the limits of the area of central Los Angeles which forms its true downtown; and only a small part of central San Diego is developed at a comparable level of intensity.

Downtown Los Angeles, through the boom periods of the early twentieth century and the twenties and thirties, limited by law from growing vertically as other American cities had done, simply expanded and grew outwards instead. Thus the character of downtown Los Angeles has historically proven so elusive because it, like the rest of the metropolitan area, has taken on an unprecedented form which simply can't be understood and appreciated, or even perceived, in terms of older city precedents or stereotypes.

IV

So here we are fresh from a high speed tour around the perimeter of Los Angeles' downtown, with its vast spread of mid and low rise structures inherited from the past and its new skyscrapers on Bunker Hill evoking images of the twenty-first century. What is it all like from within and from the viewpoint of a person on foot?

John Pastier, in his introduction to Arts and Architecture Magazine's guidemap to central Los Angeles, criticizes the new Bunker Hill financial district for its "banal and inhuman superblocks" and its lack of "genuine urbanity." Reyner Banham, in his previously mentioned chapter on downtown, describes this district as an isolated "financial ghetto complete with the huddled paranoias that go with suplete with the huddled paranoias that go with such defensive enclaves." Certainly when one looks out over Bunker Hill from the vantage of the Music Center Promenade, the size and scale of the new high-rises does indeed look superhuman, and the vast no-man's land of undeveloped territory between Bunker Hill and the old Broadway shopping district does indeed look like a hopeless barrier. But if one were instead to approach Bunker Hill from, say Sixth and Olive, starting at the remarkable James Oviatt Building, one would have an experience of an entirely different order.

V

James Oviatt's prestigious and elegant clothing emporium drew cognoscenti from all over the southland from its opening in 1929 until it closed decades later. This distinctive downtown establishment featured a Lalique glass-covered entry, elaborate deco detailing and an opulent penthouse apartment. Oviatt's attracted its devotees not in the manner of a precious jewel trapped in a field of decay, but rather as an integral part of an entire district of handsome buildings, elegant stores and high status institutions. This larger district, which one passes through on the way to Bunker Hill, has maintained its integrity and its lustre with unbroken continuity since it began to emerge after the turn of the century.

The construction of the Los Angeles Athletic Club at the corner of Seventh and Olive in 1912 marks the beginning of the district's rise. With the additions nearby of the Pacific Mutual Headquarters Building (1922,) the Biltmore Hotel (1922,) the Fine Arts Building (1925,) the Los Angeles Public Library Headquarters (1926,) and the Oviatt Building (1928) the area's status as the center of prestige in downtown was confirmed. The completion of the Richfield Building shortly later (1928) the California Club Building (1930,) the Southern California Edison Company Building (1931,) only served to fill out and reinforce a character already solidly established. More recently the 1950's additions of the Lloyd's Bank Building, the Bank of California Building, and

*"Dynamic new backdrop for One Bunker Hill..." Corner of Fifth and Grand*

several others indicate this district's continued magnetism and vitality during the period that many thought that downtown was completely disintegrating. The so-called "collapse" of downtown Los Angeles is a myth, although as with any myth there is a kernel of truth; there were several decades during which the future of downtown was very uncertain. Many of the buildings in this district are architectural achievements of high magnitude, easily comparable in quality, if not in height, with the best of the similar structures built in other American cities of the time. The design, details, materials and craftsmanship of these buildings clearly denote the quality and status of the clients that built them.

The elegant urbanity of this district has not only been continuous temporally, but it is also continuous and highly satisfying as a walking experience. At the corner of Sixth and Olive Streets, the nearly uniform cornice line of the pre-1957 buildings (generated by the height limit of 1905) does indeed create a kind of harmony and serenity that is unusual in an American downtown. This quality is enriched by the variety of styles and coloring of the different building facades, all modeled in masonry and standing uniformly right up to the sidewalk's edge. The wide projecting cornices themselves, especially those of the Biltmore Hotel and the 510 West Sixth Street Building, are of richly modeled architectural terra cotta that beckons the eye upward. The continuity of the cornice line ties together the varied facades and ceremoniously tops out the man-made environment, the blue sky beginning where cornices so elegantly end.

Beautifully maintained flourishes and embellishments, indicating pride and well-being, are all around: shop windows framed by elaborate metal filigree, dark green with the patina of age, on the 510 Building; rows of tall, robust street trees lining the sidewalks, tree trunks emerging from patterned metal grates in the pavement; elaborate cast-iron street-light standards at corners and quarter blocks; colored flags draped from projecting flag poles over the entrance to the delightful little Union Bank Building; a richly planted rooftop garden, visible from the sidewalk, at the third floor setback of the Pacific Mutual Building.

The passage from Sixth and Olive to Bunker Hill is not only abundantly rich in detail, but it also affords a progression of spatial contrasts and contrasts in scale which create a very natural and urbane transition to the dynamic power of the new Bunker Hill. The recent Crocker Bank Plaza Building on Sixth Street, visible to the west from Sixth and Olive, marks the beginning of this transition. The plaza consists of a tower resting on a four-floor tall podium which is built out to the sidewalk line and supported by a colonnade. The podium reinforces the facade continuity of the older buildings at the same time as the corner setbacks of the tower introduce the new scale and setbacks of the skyscrapers to come.

Walking west on Sixth Street and turning north on Grand, the pedestrian is surprised by Library Park, a half-block away on the left. The park suddenly opens up the spatial enclosure created by the previously continuous building facades. The park's vivid green, neatly trimmed grass, slopes slightly upward away from the viewer towards the foot of Bunker Hill, which rises up steeply just on the other side of Fifth Street from the park.

There, on the Northwest corner of Fifth and Grand, is the classic One Bunker Hill Building (formerly the Southern California Edison Company Building,) a twelve story moderne structure with a magnificent muralled lobby. This building, with its exceptional massing and corner entry detail ideally suited to its site at the foot of Bunker Hill, has traditionally marked one of the major entrances to the hill. The building served this role superbly when Bunker Hill, visibly rising in the background well above it, was a declining but fascinating neighborhood of earlier mansions crowding against later rooming houses. But One Bunker Hill serves its new, transitional role equally well -- at the same time as providing a profound sense of continuity -- with the entirely different Bunker Hill we now see towering up behind it.

Most prominent in this dynamic new backdrop is the sleek 400 South Hope Street Building and beyond that, visibly "climbing" up Bunker Hill along Grand Avenue, are the foreshortened east facades of Crocker Center's two razor edged towers. To the left, one of the skewed sides of the Security Pacific Tower, in optical illusion, appears to emerge from the side of the 400 South Hope Street Building.

Farther to the left, the top of the new Wells Fargo Building stands alone, its several setbacks prominent against the blue sky. The tower's silhouette, unlike the sensual, tangible masonry facades of the older buildings, is highly abstract and is defined by its tight skin of alternating bands of aqua-colored glazing and silver brushed stainless steel spandrel panels. Vertical panel lines are etched on the skin's surface, continuous across both glazing and spandrel, from the top of the building to the ground. This building is other-worldly indeed, but from the vantage of the pedestrian standing midblock on Grand between Fifth and Sixth, the abstract tower rises above and appears to grow out of the humane intimacy of Library Park's lush green grass and vegetation.

Directly across Fifth Street from this park, and prominently visible at street level, is a sparse, buff-colored retaining wall increasing dramatically in height to the left as Bunker Hill rises steeply westward from the wall's starting point at Fifth and Grand. This wall, with the One Bunker Hill Building (both designed and constructed together to enhance the development of this site,) form an ensemble which is one of the most dramatic and compelling features of the entire downtown cityscape. In fact, this grouping is a textbook-perfect example of a "city seam," celebrating the exact point of transition between two distinct but related urban districts at the same time as it subtly but effectively ties the two districts together.

Just off Fifth and Grand, in front of One Bunker Hill and supported by the retaining wall, is a narrow spur street connecting this intersection with Hope Street high above, which terminates abruptly at the top of the retaining wall. With all the powerful, futuristic images beckoning, a walk up this steep street is irresistably inviting.

At the corner of Fifth and Grand, where the spur begins, is the imposing main entrance to One Bunker Hill. This entry is an unenclosed but covered space several floors tall, carved from the corner of the building and capped by a dome of elaborately carved and colored surfaces, visible in the shadows high above as the viewer looks from within. A short distance farther up the hill are windows, affording a glimpse of the building's opulent lobby. Next door and halfway up the steep climb is the old, gray Engstrom Apartment Building with its pattern of cantilevered

*"This enormous, gleaming towering monolith..." Wells Fargo Building (1982, A. C. Martin & Associates, architects)*

wrought-iron balconies, a wonderful relic from and reminder Bunker Hill as it was. Visible ahead, just over the crest of th hill, the silver-green east facade of the Wells Fargo Tower shoo upwards, drawing the eye of the viewer up to the sky. A fe steps farther to the top and... SMASH! There it is, full blow immediately in front of you -- this gleaming towering monolith.

From this point, at the threshold of the Wells Fargo Building ar the other new Bunker Hill developments, one can turn to the le and look over the guardrail at the end of Hope Street, to Librar Park and another world below. The old landmarks -- the Biltmor Hotel, the Pacific Mutual Building and the Library, which we on just passed -- all seem suddenly far away, and the transition fro the past to the present is complete.

Turning again to face the Wells Fargo Building, one begins a electrifying descent down the other side of Bunker Hill, throug the open base of the tower, and into the new financial district. series of steep escalators modulates the descent as the viewe passes cool waterfalls, stepped terraces, and green marbl columns which support the tower overhead. The descer terminates at a handsomely paved plaza which emerges from th shade of the tower above, into the sun at the corner of Fifth ar Flower, the heart of the new financial district.

VII

The experience just described compares favorably with a walkir tour of any of the more celebrated urban settings in America. takes in, however, only the smallest part of the many extensiv complex and historically rich sub-districts that compri downtown Los Angeles. To anyone who finds pleasure in urba life but who is unfamiliar with Los Angeles and unburdened by th literature and mythology which have built up around it, a tou through the larger downtown area would be a joy.

# SAH/SCC Membership

# Vol·III·No.1·Winter·1984

*Editor:* Richard Rowe
*Assistant Editor:* Lynn Bryant
*Photographic Editor:* Bruce Boehner
*Publications Committee:* Bruce Boehner, Lynn Bryant, Donna Harris, Diann Marsh, Karen Safer Polich, Mary Power, Richard Rowe, Kathryn Smith, & Bob Young
*This Issue's Contributors:* Bruce Boehner, Candida Burke, Susan Hensley, Karen Safer Polich & Richard Rosen
*Graphics/Production:* Carlos Figueroa
*Printing:* Nugent Printing, Pasadena

SOCIETY OF ARCHITECTURAL HISTORIANS/SOUTHERN CALIFORNIA CHAPTER

## 1983/84 OFFICERS AND EXECUTIVE BOARD

VIRGINIA KAZOR, President, 221 S Wilton Pl., LA, CA 90004 — 660-2200
PAULINE STEIN, Vice-President, 1156 San Ysidro Dr., B. Hills, CA 90210 — 275-0497
MICHAEL DOUGHERTY, Secretary, 2535 E Chevy Chase Dr., Glendale, CA 91206 — 974-1901
STAN PENTON, Treasurer, 1087 Moraga Dr., LA, CA 90049 — 476-1855
SUSAN HENSLEY, Preservation Officer, 3737 Fredonia Dr., LA, CA 90068 — 459-2306
Executive Board:
BRUCE BOEHNER, 231 N Union, LA, CA 90026 — 245-1044
ALSON CLARK, 430 Lakeview Road, Pasadena, CA 91105 — 743-2798
RICHARD ROWE, 239 N Orange Grove, Pasadena, CA 91103 — 977-1660

ur LOCAL chapter is affiliated with the National Society of Architectural Historians, but requires separate membership dues. Although we encourage our local chapter members to also be members of the National Chapter, it is NOT a pre-requisite of local membership. The SAH/SCC organizes educational programs, events, tours, and lectures. The SAH/SCC publishes the AH/SCC REVIEW three times annually and the SAH/SCC NEWSLETTER bimonthly.

LOCAL SAH/SCC MEMBERSHIP: Individual, $12 per year; Couple, $18 per year (one mailing); and Life, one-time contribution of $150. Membership is obtained by sending a note with your current mailing address and your check (payable to AH/SCC) to SAH/SCC Chapter Secretary, c/o The Gamble House, 4 Westmoreland Place, Pasadena, CA 91103 -- (213) 81-6427 or (818) 793-3334. Although The Gamble House is our mailing address, we have no staff to answer calls there. The Gamble House docent answering the phone may have SAH/SCC event information, but any other question will be referred to a current officer for an answer.

III

have asserted that downtown Los Angeles is the preeminent center of metropolitan status and culture in Southern California. Banham asserts that "most of what is contained within the confines of (the central freeway loop) could disappear overnight and the bulk of the citizenry would never even notice." And everyone all over the world has heard of Hollywood and Beverly Hills, but... downtown Los Angeles?

The fact is that because of the unusual circumstances of Los Angeles' development, both Banham's and my assertions are true. There is here a class of citizens which does form both the mercantile and civic backbone of the metropolis, or more precisely, which does have a good deal of power over people's lives and a tremendous impact on what happens here. It is this class primarily which has both created and enjoyed the districts of downtown described herein. But at the same time, the growth of

the metropolitan area has been so sudden and so explosive, and the interests of the burgeoning populace have been generally so non-urban, that downtown activities truly seem irrelevant to the vast majority of Angelenos and have consequently remained invisible to them. And because the form of the metropolis resulting from these unusual circumstances was so different from the professional planners' and historians' ideal, Victor Gruen, along with scores of other critics over the decades, lashed out, condemning that form, regardless of its actual appearance.

The fact that people are unaware of something or unwilling to see it does not mean that it does not exist. The center of Los Angeles is downtown; it most definitely does exist, and it tells a fascinating and marvelous story -- in the most articulate of terms -- to anyone who chooses to take the time to listen. ■

*The old landmarks all seem suddenly far away..." View over the guardrail at the foot of Hope Street*

*Entry detail, Warner Brothers Western Theatre (now Wiltern Theatre)/Pellissier Building (1930–31, Morgan, Walls & Clements, architects with G. A. Landsburgh and Anthony B. Heinsbergen) Photo: Bruce Boehner.*

SOCIETY OF ARCHITECTURAL HISTORIANS / SOUTHERN CALIFORNIA CHAPTER ■ C/O THE GAMBLE HOUSE, 4 Westmoreland Place, Pasadena CA 9110

SOCIETY · OF · ARCHITECTURAL · HISTORIANS
UTILICITAS
FIRMITAS
VENUSTAS
OS · 1940 · SU